THE BLUEPRINT FOR A SUCCESSFUL CAREER

A Foundation for Developing Young Professionals

Will Baggett, M.Ed.

with

Tai M. Brown, M.Ed.

Forward Management © Tai M. Brown (Registration Number: TXu 2-081-385). Used with permission.

ISBN: 978-1-60679-364-0
Library of Congress Control Number: 2016949724
Cover design: Onesimus Williams & Evan Wooten
Book layout: Cheery Sugabo
Front cover photo: © 123rf.com
Back cover photo: www.photodune.net
Illustrations: MariaTkach/iStock/Thinkstock (Yin Yang symbol in Diagrams 1 and 2); Dorling Kindersley/Thinkstock (Diagram 3)

Coaches Choice
P.O. Box 1828
Monterey, CA 93942
www.coacheschoice.com

Dedication

For my parents, who taught me the power of love, perseverance, and Christian values. To my beloved English teacher, Mrs. Charlene Leverette, who encouraged me to become a pro at prose. Your legacy lives on through these lines.

"O Captain! My Captain…"

—Will Baggett

Acknowledgments

As I do every day, I wish to first acknowledge my Lord and Savior Jesus Christ. I am but one of many vessels through which He speaks. I also wish to acknowledge you, the reader. Thank you for giving me a chance to share my passion, and I hope you are empowered to go out and excel in everything you do. Colossians 3:23 reads: And whatsoever ye do, do it heartily, as to the Lord, and not unto men.

—W.B.

Foreword

Will Baggett and Tai M. Brown have arresting personalities. As I got ready to read their book, I thought back over our shared history and was surprised by the sheer number of instances I recalled in which one or the other had popped up in my life. Such a situation is not all that unusual, since I am busy, and we move in similar circles. There is something in this instance, however, that is unusual: I remember each encounter...and when I do, I smile.

What is that? I have many recollections of Will and Tai, and, without exception, they are positive. No matter the setting, these two guys made me feel better about myself every single time. I should add here that I am at an age (73) at which my "flattery detector" (there is another locker room term for this, but we are in polite company) is highly sensitive and 100 percent accurate. I will remove myself from my immediate surroundings if I sense that I am being patronized. Neither of these individuals has ever done that.

When teaching or writing about leadership, I start with the premise that each human being is a leader. Whenever someone enters a group, the energy automatically changes. The group either experiences a spurt from a fountain of positive energy, or a drain from the negativity. Each person decides each day what their leadership will be for that day. Regardless of our circumstances, each of us can make all the difference with that choice. Thus, my definition: "A real leader is a consistent, powerful, positive presence." Will Baggett and Tai M. Brown are leaders!

When such people write, they do so for the benefit of others, hoping to let their light shine through the darkness of our very selfish era. Will and Tai's hopes for just that are realized in this book. In the interest of space, and so that I do not write another book in the front of this one, I have compiled a list of just a few of my notes. Look for them, and you will not only learn, but will also have fun:

- All of the suggestions in this book are sound, and while you may have seen some of them before, you will have never seen them this cleverly organized.
- Sources range from philosophy to religion, from the pool room (8 ball—solids or stripes) to kid's toys (bop bags), from John Wayne ("Hold it there, Tex.") to Robert Frost, from the construction site (foundations matter!) to the weight room. Furthermore, their advice sticks.
- The modern world of information technology is reviewed and enhanced ("Override the auto-generated message with a personal one!").
- The unifying message of paying attention to the process is never out of sight, and is vividly reinforced in an entertaining way on virtually every page.

You will enjoy reading the work of these very bright individuals. In the process, you will gain vivid word pictures firmly implanted in your mind that will stay with you for life.

Who knows, maybe your influence will outlive you, and you may even find yourself writing Will and Tai a handwritten letter.

> —Bill Curry
> Former Head Coach (NFL and College)
> Two-time SEC Coach of the Year
> Super Bowl Champion (Player, Super Bowl I)

Contents

Preface

*"If I have seen further than other
men, it is by standing on the
shoulders of giants."*

—Sir Isaac Newton

If you have experienced any measure of success in your personal
or professional life, you are likely indebted to a giant in one way or
another. This metaphorical giant is likened to someone who has
reached a career stature which enables him to see above and beyond
a typical sightline. Thus, the benefit a person stands to gain from being
given a leg-up by one of these figures can certainly go a long way.

Nevertheless, as I read up on prominent individuals, more often
than not, I find myself slightly underwhelmed. While their many
accomplishments are certainly worthy of acclaim, I find myself
constantly inquiring about the colossal-like individuals who positively
impacted their lives and careers. Who showed them the way? Who
corrected their early mistakes? Whom do they continue to call upon for
advice before making big decisions?

Unfortunately, the names of these giants—the individuals who
allowed for such deep shoulder impressions—never seem to make
the final editor's cut. Nevertheless, I'm willing to bet the subjects of
these write-ups would relish the opportunity to give their respective
giants their due recognition. How such behemoths are consistently
overlooked is beyond me, but that does not mean this trend cannot
be reversed. It begins now. I realize I would be bereft of vital elements
of professional acumen if not for the individuals who offered their time
and resources. *The Blueprint* was crafted as a token of my appreciation
for these individuals, as well as a means of sharing the wealth of
knowledge I have gained from them over the years.

As millennials, there is no shortage of knocks against us and our outlook as rising professionals. I am probably mincing words when I say employers collectively view us as entitled whippersnappers, yearning for instant-gratification. A bit harsh, eh? My contention is that we are perfectly capable of carrying the torch, but like the generations before us, we will require some guidance.

Before we chart the course, however, we must first identify the root cause of the issues at hand to better understand where we need to go and what will ultimately lead us down the desired path. Maybe the manner in which mentors share the essentials have not adapted to the times, or perhaps we, as millennials, have not been as receptive to the teachings as we ought.

My assumption is that it is a combination of both scenarios. In either case, therein lies an issue that, if not addressed, will cripple our workforce. Recognizing the realistic possibility of this situation occurring further prompted this book. Hopefully, the manner in which we present the essentials will begin bridging the ever-widening gap between the interdependent cohorts.

We, as aspiring professionals, must acknowledge that our higher-ups have likely forgotten more than we will ever know in some aspects. Conversely, we offer a variety of fresh perspectives, grounded in innovation and technological savviness. Should we make a collective effort to espouse the two knowledge bases, it will really make for something special. In an effort to begin this process, I felt inclined to share the wisdom imparted by some of the leading figures in my beloved profession of sport. Because sport is regarded as the world's greatest outdoor classroom, I am confident the writings presented in this book may benefit those in other disciplines. This guide is designed to provide insight for how you may gain a competitive advantage as a young professional.

Growing up, my father—a construction manager—would always take me to work with him when I was out on summer break. I vividly recall those Mississippi summer days spent at his side on various job sites, usually sporting one of his oversized caps.

I quickly learned that, like anything else, there is a process to building a house. Though he would oversee each phase of his construction projects intently, first and foremost, he placed particular emphasis on perfecting the foundation. As we labored to prepare each lot, he would look over at me and say, "Lil' Will, this is the key player in the game. We have one shot at this thing. If we don't get the foundation right, we won't be able to build on it."

This approach should be applied to the start of your professional tenure. How you approach your first professional opportunity will lay the groundwork for the remainder of your career. If the provenance of your career begins on a weak foundation, it will inevitably catch up with you. Any homeowner who has ever had his house foundation settle and shift on its base will tell you that such an occurrence essentially offsets the entire structure. The outward appearance may remain intact, but because corners were cut in establishing the foundation, everything that was built upon it will be grossly affected. It is only a matter of time before it begins to show on the outside.

Your career could face a similar fate, if it is not firmly established on solid ground. The chapters to follow provide strategies to assist you in beginning your career on a sturdy platform. In this way, all that will be required of you is to continually build upon it—absent the worry that your base of support could possibly settle and offset your framework.

Let's say, for instance, you begin full-time employment in your 20s. You will amass, at minimum, 40 years of professional experience in accordance with the length of a traditional career. With your goals and ambitions in full focus, the last thing you should be concerned with is replacing your foundation year after year. The concepts detailed in this book will help ensure that establishing a robust foundation is a one-time ordeal so you may focus your full attention on building a successful career.

In electing to begin this project, it became apparent that relatively few young professionals are afforded the caliber of mentorship from which I am blessed to benefit. I'm referencing a grade of mentorship that supersedes the status quo and catapults into a stratosphere of selfless guidance. The portal to such a realm was made accessible to me in large part by a core group of extraordinary influencers. The foremost of which, Tai M. Brown, graciously agreed to assist me with this effort. Tai's (pronounced "tie") leadership philosophy is predicated on creating and maintaining an environment of which people want to be a part.

His input is interspersed throughout the text to corroborate the concepts that are shared from a young professional's standpoint with intuitive insight from an organizational leadership perspective. This dual-wielded method effectively eliminates the grey area that often persists with writings crafted from a single vantage point. In other words, this book is not intended to stare at you from behind a two-way mirror, as your industry plays good cop, bad cop.

It is my sincere hope these lessons will be as beneficial for you as they have been for me and that you will share this information with others throughout your career. The very livelihood and forward progression of our workforce depends on it. Similarly, although my name is printed on the front cover, I recognize I would be remiss to stake claim as the sole architect of this body of knowledge. I was, however, sent to deliver *The Blueprint.*

—W.B.

Forward Management:
Developing Young Professionals

© Tai M. Brown

Forward Management (FM) is an organizational leadership philosophy that, when implemented, leads to professional growth amongst your employees and contributes to the overall productivity of your organization. The premise of Forward Management originates from the following principles:

A. The role of a leader is to create and maintain an environment that people want to be a part of.

B. If you are an effective leader, those you lead will go on to become effective leaders themselves.

When applied properly, FM can also lead to the successful transformation of those new to the workforce—from entry-level employees to experienced young professionals. However, before you continue reading, ask yourself the following question: Are you leading for your own success, or are you leading to develop other leaders?

While there is no right or wrong answer, consider taking the question a step further: "How can you create and maintain a successful environment that people want to be a part of, while simultaneously helping those within that environment develop into effective leaders?" Essentially, success in both endeavors can lead to prosperity for your organization while concurrently promoting care for the personal and professional well-being of those under your guidance. Further, if you do your job well as a leader, those you lead will represent you in a positive manner as they go on to become leaders themselves. With these points in mind, the environment you create must be conducive to teaching an individual to be both productive and enterprising.

Forward Management is rooted in accountability and the concept of expectation-with-evaluation. To ensure clarity, it is necessary to define accountability in the context of FM. Accountability is two-fold; it is the responsibility of the individual for the actions of the whole, in addition to the responsibility of the whole for the actions of the individual. Essentially, accountability is the glue that keeps a team together.

The concept of expectation-with-evaluation isn't new but to understand its practicality within Forward Management, it's worth explaining. Much of the success in leading others, as well as leading ourselves, stems from our ability to understand and explain the responsibilities inherent to our respective positions. Taking this a step further, the essential ingredient that gives people the opportunity to be successful in an industrious environment is a complete comprehension of how those aforementioned responsibilities will be evaluated. And when combined with a frequent and consistent evaluation process, the fusion of accountability with expectations, applied within the Forward Management framework, creates a workplace positioned for prosperity.

Forward Management is divided into three phases. Each phase represents a stage in the personal and/or professional development of those you lead.

Phase #1 – Creation: Create an environment for your staff to be successful
Phase #2 – Cultivation: Maintain this environment through the cultivation of good Hab1ts*
Phase #3 – Affirmation: Affirm your staff as they have proven to be assets to you and your organization

Phase #1: Creation
Create an environment for your staff to be successful

1. Why – *Why do we do what we do?* The first step to creating a productive and enterprising environment is to ensure you have a simply stated purpose for your team, unit, department, organization, or company. "The purpose" keeps those you lead focused on why they do what they do.

2. Buy-In – *Is working for you more than just another paycheck?* Help your new hires embrace the company culture by showing them why their position is an important function of helping your team successfully fulfill its purpose. Beyond that, people inherently want to know, "What is in it for me?" In order for your staff to buy what you are selling, you

*Hab1ts = One thing, one percent better, one day at a time.

must also help them understand how they as individuals will benefit, personally and professionally, through the process of fulfilling the purpose.

3. Descriptive Expectations – *How will you evaluate your staff?* Now that you have made the hire, you'll need to explain the responsibilities of the position, and more importantly, define the standards of performance for how you expect the job to be done. Effectively doing these two things leaves no grey area when it comes time for staff evaluations because by doing so, you have essentially laid the foundation for organizational accountability. You'll find that after defining expectations and explaining responsibilities, people will do one of the following four things: 1). Do the job; 2). Excel at the job; 3). Choose not to do the job; or 4). Realize they don't have the ability to perform the job.

4. Dutiful Duties – *Does your staff know why each job is important?* The big picture is made up of many small pictures, therefore, extraordinary execution on the small scale allows for exceptional execution on the large scale. If you have explained how everything ties to the purpose, then you should be able to explain how each assignment—whether large or small—has a role in successfully fulfilling that purpose.

Phase #2: Cultivation
Maintain this environment through the cultivation of good Hab1ts*

5. Internal Comparison – *Be better tomorrow than you are today: Don't compare yourself to the person next to you; compare yourself to the person you were yesterday.* Create a measurable—a frequent and consistent internal, personal evaluation process—so people can measure themselves against themselves. By incorporating this practice of incremental benchmarking, the members of your staff will come to realize they have made significant strides over a designated time period. Once internal comparison becomes a habit, then allow for external competition amongst the staff and/or those in similar positions throughout the industry.

6. Responsive Feedback – *People want to know their input is heard and potentially useful.* Encourage input from your staff. By doing so, they feel they have a say in the project you are building. Help them help you by doing the following: 1). Listen to their ideas;

Hab1ts = One thing, one percent better, one day at a time.

2). Provide feedback on their ideas; 3). Determine if their ideas can be implemented; and 4). If one of them can be implemented, proceed to implement it. Allowing your employees to have input in important decisions will lead them to further embrace the company culture.

7. Productive Motivation Cycle – *Productivity breeds motivation.* Create frequent and consistent evaluation tools for measuring productivity so your staff can see how their accomplishments help to fulfill the purpose. When people see positive results from their efforts, they are motivated to continue producing those results. Also, if you have successfully shown how fulfilling the purpose will help them in their personal and professional development, they will then be motivated by an even stronger stimulant—their own success.

Phase #3: Affirmation
Affirm your staff as they have proven
to be assets to you and your organization

8. Employee Recognition – *People want to feel valued.* If your staff has excelled at the job you have defined for them, exceeded the expectations you have laid out for them, provided valuable input on projects, and proven to be a productive asset, then you should recognize their contribution to the fulfillment of the purpose. Recognizing your staff as part of the reason for the team's success helps to foster a productive and enterprising culture they will embrace as a significant milestone in their career.

9. Do You Fit My Jersey – *Can your staff walk in public with a jersey that has your name on the back of it?* Accountability. Your staff represents you. Do you feel comfortable sending them out into the world with your reputation in their hands? If you have done your job in creating and maintaining an accountable, desirable, productive, and enterprising environment, then your staff should represent you well.

10. Walk With the Elephants – *Would you bring your staff around influential leaders in the industry?* In order to be successful, you must walk with the elephants. This can be rephrased as, in order to be successful, you must be around successful people. Elephants are big, imposing animals that everyone notices. In every industry, there are influential leaders who are considered the elephants of the profession.

In every industry, there are influential leaders who are considered the elephants of the profession.

Learning from these leaders happens best when you are amongst them. As you have trained your staff to wear your jersey comfortably, allow them to accompany you as you walk with the elephants of your industry.

11. Putting It Back in the Bucket – *Is your staff ready to mentor others as you have mentored them?* Dipping in the proverbial bucket of experience and mentorship helped you get to where you are today. You have given back to that bucket by helping others to be successful through creating and maintaining an environment for leadership development. To ensure a similar outcome, teach this concept to your staff so that when they become leaders, they too will create and maintain their own environment for successful leadership.

Throughout this book, the tenets of Forward Management are strategically placed to highlight the leadership perspective relative to the lesson communicated in the text. For those of us who find ourselves in the influential position of leading young professionals, we must accept the charge of helping them to be better tomorrow than they are today.

—Tai M. Brown
Positive Energy

P.S. The key to a peaceful existence is to master the ability to <u>Adjust Accordingly.</u>

Pre-Game

Annual commencement ceremonies across the country serve as floodgates to a burgeoning labor force of young professionals who are seeking to gain ground in their careers. Surely, you have heard folktales about when having a mere college degree would all but guarantee a person a job. Those are days, however, that we as millennials can only dream about.

As the concentration of skilled young professionals continues to blossom, so does the number of job applications that need to be removed from the short stack (for one reason or another) to improve your chances of being selected. Upon completion of my undergraduate studies, I was under the impression a high grade point average would all but guarantee consideration for most positions. I quickly learned, however, that this notion was a myth.

The knee-jerk reaction for a person is to assign blame to the strength of their network when that individual is passed over for an opening. While this line of thinking may hold some validity, it is likely a small fragment in a larger holding of potential shortcomings. While it would violate every law of professional development to speak against the importance of growing your network, I caution you to first ensure that you are fully prepared to optimize your efforts to expand your network. Begin by asking yourself the following questions: Do you add value to someone's existing network? Is it a mutually beneficial relationship? Or, do you just need a job? This continuum of consideration spans the poles of professionalism and thus should be taken into account when contemplating new relationships.

While you may have lofty career goals, the "secret stuff" required to make you like Mike is not found in the chapters in this book. What they do speak to, however, is the process. This process involves foundational maxims and strategies that make for a smooth transition from pupil to professional. (Note: I would have thrown "from backpacks to briefcases" in to keep the alliteration juices flowing, but I'm still lugging my backpack around as a full-time employee.)

As we delve into these topics, consider conducting a self-audit on your career goals. In what are they truly grounded? Money, power, prestige, or a combination of all of the aforementioned? There was one particular instance in which I overheard a conversation between an established sport professional and a graduate assistant coach. The former asked the graduate assistant what his career goals were. He quickly replied, "I want to be the head football coach at a Division 1 FBS institution."

The professional followed up with the simple question, "Why?", and the young coach quickly found himself at a loss for words. I am hard-pressed to believe he had set his goal mere days before, yet and still, a one-word inquiry caught him off guard. With respect to that profession and other high-ranking positions alike, I would advise any individual with similar goals to have an answer ready—a good one. Fortunately for the graduate student, there was nothing at stake the first time someone posed the question "Why?" to him in response to his career aspirations. Or was there? (Caution: You never truly know when your job interviews commence. In fact, you are *always* interviewing.) Although the question "Why?" is elementary in nature, your response to it could determine the trajectory of your career from that point forward.

As evidenced by the Venn diagram detailed in Diagram 1, "Why?" is the interconnected area that syncs the relationship between what you do and how you go about doing it. Absent a purpose, the circles become mutually exclusive. For example, consider each circle to be independent and representative of the two sides of an everyday coin. Unless you carry a double-sided coin like the Gotham character Two-Face in the comic Batman, if you were to flip it, you would end up with either heads or tails.

Referee officials follow this procedure in football to determine which team will earn the right to receive or defer the opening kickoff. This method of determining "which one" signifies a lack of shared

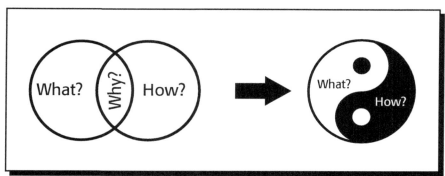

Diagram 1. Venn diagram illustrating the interconnected relationship between what you do and how you go about doing it

interest outside of defeating the opposition, or simply collaborating only to compete. One team will begin on the offensive side of the ball, with the other on defense by default. In other words, the positioning of the teams, as well as the start of the contest, hinges on one side of a measly coin.

On the other hand, if you were to factor in the "Why?", the faces of that decisive coin would begin to resemble a Yin Yang symbol. The shaded areas of the Yin Yang, representative of "What?" and "How?", may appear different, but they share equal face value. As such, they complement one another to achieve wholeness. Furthermore, each side of the Yin Yang houses smaller circles in the likeness of the "opposing" side. The presence and positioning of these circles conveys an apparent sense of interdependence among the regions.

In similar fashion, the space each small circle occupies on the Yin Yang infuses contralateral value into what would otherwise be regarded as independent functions, i.e. what you do and how you do it. If you were to draw a line through the circles, it would travel right down the middle. Likewise, if you were to slide the Yin Yang into the center of the Venn diagram as shown in Diagram 2, the circles would fit perfectly into the interlocking region. At this point, these circles fully inhabit the "Why?" sector, and rightfully so, given that both the Venn diagram and Yin Yang rely on mutualism to achieve oneness.

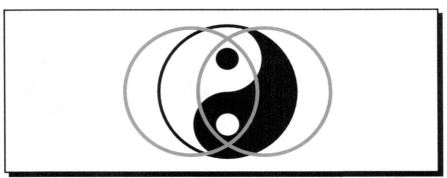

Diagram 2. An illustration of Yin Yang slid into the center of the Venn diagram, represented in Diagram 1

The visual shown in Diagram 2 objectifies the principle that two heads are better than one, especially when they are on the same side. Thus, the "Why?" territory is solidified as the intersection of influence between what you do and the manner of how you go about doing it. It must be defined. Why? Because your "Why?" holds the key to the internal gateway that will unlock your full potential.

Still not convinced? Using the image detailed in Diagram 2, place your index fingers at either of the points at which the circles of the Venn diagram intersect and begin to trace the curved lines, until they depart from the combined image. Then, take the shape you have just outlined and turn it sideways. You come up with the image detailed in Diagram 3.

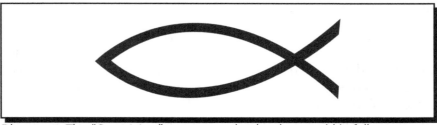

Diagram 3. The "Great I Am," or purpose that has been paid in full

Before you read any further, be honest with yourself and ask yourself why you have set a particular career goal. If the answer does not impress you, I guarantee that it will not impress anyone seeking to make a new hire—regardless of the level of the position you are seeking.

Discouraged? Don't be. The good news is you have time. Just think, if you can begin to define your "Why?" early on in your career, imagine how your future experiences will further mold that definition as you grow in your field. As such, you will then have something of substance to strive for outside of external rewards. By the time you are ready to apply for a position, your motives for securing that role will be so impressive that it will have prospective employers questioning why they themselves ever entered the profession!

The Blueprint – Leadership Perspective

Forward Management (© Tai M. Brown)

❏ **PHASE #1: CREATION**
(Create an environment for your staff to be successful.)

1. Why – *Why do we do what we do?* The first step to creating a productive and enterprising environment is to ensure you have a simply stated purpose for your team, unit, department, organization, or company. "The purpose" keeps those you lead focused on why they do what they do.

PART I
The Lay of the Land

CHAPTER 1
Buy Your Way In

*"Don't you ever get to thinking
you're irreplaceable."*

—Beyoncé

Hold it there, Tex. Before you begin flaunting your best poker face, it is important to understand what organizational buy-in actually entails. Organizational buy-in is the principle that promotes transcendence concerning how you approach day-to-day responsibilities. It mitigates any monotony new hires may experience by presenting a notable distinction between excelling—as opposed to merely existing—in their roles. Accordingly, buy-in may be depicted as the first rung on which an individual must establish footing to begin climbing the proverbial ladder.

Whether serving as a volunteer, intern, or even beginning in a full-time role, buying-in is the key to avoiding stagnation in your work environment. During the onboarding process, you will go through an orientation phase in which human resources will provide a rundown of workplace policies and procedures. While important, be forewarned: *this phase does not establish buy-in!* Although this stage is an integral component of the onboarding process, the takeaways will be centered primarily on office etiquette. If you are *not* seeking upward mobility, this information alone will likely suffice for you. Go right ahead; just do what is outlined on your job description like everyone else. On the other hand, you should know you have an alternative.

When you begin working in a new position, subconsciously, your first objective tends to be to assure your leader that he did not make a mistake by hiring you. You initiate this process by doing the little things that will help demonstrate your value and commitment to the company. From fluffing the lobby pillows to distributing mints in the restroom, no job appears to be too small at the time. This approach lasts for the first few weeks or so. Or, until you get affirmation from your leader that who you professed to be in your interview was not just a façade. This proving period is a phase many new hires give way to, but one that usually comes to an unceremonious end as a sense of comfort begins to settle in. Make no mistake; this phase is the most critical juncture of the onboarding process. It is where, as renowned poet Robert Frost describes it, two roads diverge in a wood. (Caution: Do not rest on the laurels of these woods.)

It is at this point that you contemplate if you are willing to go above and beyond or, if only doing the bare minimum will keep you off the chopping block. As time goes on, you begin to convince yourself the lobby pillows do not require fluffing *every* day and that your coworkers are perfectly capable of grabbing their own mints in the restroom. You can activate cruise control now, comforted in knowing the vessel is at least moving forward, and all you have to do is steady the ship. You must remain mindful; however, that failure to move the needle is what ultimately allows colleagues and competitors alike to bypass those who have set cruise control on the path to success. This consideration begs the question: Are you playing to win or not to lose?

The aforementioned comfort zone is a safety net many of us fall into, and it's a doozy. This net is so well-disguised that you can be oblivious to the extent of its entanglement capabilities. You may even wrongfully perceive it as a hammock that was strung for your comfort and enjoyment. This mindset is the road most traveled and the antithesis of buying-in to your leader and place of employment. It is a road filled with speedbumps to reduce your work performance and sinkholes lined with warning signs that read: "That's not my job." Once you find yourself in the trenches, your only hope is for the little helper from Mario Kart to fish out your vehicle and reset it on the proper course. We have all been there.

You do, however, have the option of avoiding this pitfall altogether by embracing the proving period, not as a finite timeframe, but as a way of life. You should make a conscious decision to sustain the attitude of a perennial prover, whether or not it is acknowledged by others.

In any case, you will have to show your worth by initially completing assignments you may regard as menial. Buying-in, however, keeps you mindful of the fact you are contributing to the overall success of your organization. Thus, such undertakings begin to take on all-new meaning and value. We all have biased perceptions of our proficiencies beyond our job titles, especially as young professionals. As a result, this can be quite the humbling experience—but necessary nonetheless. The question remains, however, how do you go about showing the extent of your competencies once you have your foot in the door?

For starters, consider looking at the full exhibit of your organization's picture-perfect-purpose, and then identifying where your personal thumbnails fit into each portrait of the gallery. Similar to photography, the "negatives" you may perceive about your job are what will ultimately be used to develop the clear image of the organization. Thus, it is imperative to grasp an understanding of how your role contributes to the bigger picture through multiple lenses.

The following example outlines how you can go about accomplishing this feat. Along with your standard responsibilities at Banana Tech, you are also responsible for vending services. You get the snacks; you stock the machine. Nothing to see here, right? On the contrary, my dear Watson!

There are certain steps you can take to ascertain the underlying value of the assignment, for example:

- Evaluate the buying trends and revenue generated by the existing selections.

- Discern if there is displeasure among your coworkers with the current options.

- If so, design and distribute surveys to determine what options your coworkers would like and make every effort to secure them.

If you do not work directly in customer service or marketing, you now have experience in these areas to document on your résumé. Such mention is not just lip-service, or rather keyboard-service, in this case. In reality, it worked for me. The aforementioned scenario is an exact interpretation of a responsibility I was given as a graduate assistant and elected to optimize. Prior to my oversight of the operation, few in the office even knew that our organization offered vending services, due to the lack of options.

It goes without saying that little-to-no revenue was being generated to boot. In fact, the vending machine was not even earning its keep if you factor in its contribution to the electric bill. Knowing that vending revenue would hardly decide whether we operated in the red or black, this was my first opportunity to take ownership, so I approached it as though it would. By undertaking the aforementioned steps, I was, in fact, able to significantly increase the vending revenue and later assumed the title, Director of Vending Services.

We are all susceptible to feelings of devaluation in the workplace. It happens on occasion to everyone who is not actually in charge of a particular project. For this reason, it is imperative to take responsible ownership of whatever is entrusted to you—no matter how miniscule the task may seem. In doing so, you will fortify your morale and sustain a high degree of mettle. By going above and beyond with small responsibilities of your own, you bring the extent of your talents to the forefront in the process. This outcome is due in part to your leader actively noticing that you are willing to do whatever, whenever to advance the organization.

The Blueprint – Leadership Perspective

Forward Management (© Tai M. Brown)

❏ **PHASE #1: CREATION**

2. Buy-In – *Is working for you more than just another paycheck?* Help your new hires embrace the company culture by showing them why their position is an important function of helping your team successfully fulfill its purpose. Beyond that, people inherently want to know, "What is in it for me?" In order for your staff to buy what you are selling, you must also help them understand how they as individuals will benefit, personally and professionally, through the process of fulfilling the purpose.

In addition, you will soon be entrusted with greater responsibilities because: Say the following with me: "People don't care how much you know until they know how much you _____." Exactly.

Your leader will be in awe of your genuine care for a given undertaking, one that everyone assigned to it before you either took for granted or completely disregarded. At this point, the bar is set and anything below it will be perceived as a *lack* of care or utter insubordination.

Arguably, your leader will take on the following mindset regarding your work ethic: *"If he takes small assignments this seriously, imagine what he will do when granted a much greater assignment?"* Even if it does not immediately reach this particular frame of mind, your leader will, at a minimum, have anecdotal evidence to share with a prospective employer about you, should he be called upon to check a reference. This concept is further addressed in Chapter 7—Jersey Swap.

Adopting a work ethic of this nature will be regarded as specific to you and can serve to increase your value as you climb the ladder. If you master the ability to self-manage as a young professional and compound it with a resolute work ethic, you will begin to crack and ultimately shatter any glass ceiling that may be confronting you. In fact, the primary reason rising professionals are stymied by the glass ceiling effect is that they have become too high and mighty to dab it with a little Windex every now and again. Furthermore, similar to the toothpaste-covered bathroom mirror we often neglect to clean, our vision can become somewhat obscured as a result.

The following saying has considerable merit, "What got you to where you are will not get you to where you want to be." Sort of. As you progress in your career, you will naturally acquire new skills and responsibilities. On the other hand, if you use these newly-acquired talents to merely supplant your original expertise, you will only move from one glass pane to another. Instead, you should continue adding new layers to your existing skillset as you work to achieve the professional goals you have set for yourself.

Once you begin approaching every task as if it is of utmost importance, you will find yourself performing at levels that may even surprise you. You will begin doing the little things that people notice but cannot seem to trace, and that is A-OK. Receiving credit and adulation should not be your objective. You should be concerned with being better tomorrow than you are today. Make a concerted effort to do one thing, 1 percent better, one day at a time.

As another saying states, "You are your own biggest critic." How about taking that critique a step further en route to becoming your own biggest *competitor*? Did you take an "L" against yesterday's version of yourself?

Frankly, I have to admit that I have taken my fair share of "Ls"— primarily because I was benchmarking my performance against other individuals, instead of my own standards. Each of us possesses natural gifts and talents that may allow for us to sometimes hold back, yet still yield acceptable results. This factor was my Achilles heel for the longest time. In other words, a mediocre effort on my part would sometimes be equivalent to or greater than that of a peer in a given endeavor. During that period, I honestly thought this approach was alright—mainly because I was being rewarded for it in some shape or form. Can you relate?

As a suffering perfectionist, it was tough to accept that my best effort was not always well…perfect. Perhaps, that is why I would sometimes stop short—so I could maintain some form of quasi-dignity if I did not get it quite right. As time went on, however, I soon encountered a number of instances that required everything I had in the tank and then some. By that time, however, I'd already trained my mind to do just enough to be among the best, as opposed to striving to be the best.

After undergoing a mentality transformation, primarily while under Tai's direction and through my work as an athletic performance coach, I realized how big of a problem this manner of doing things was and how much time and potential I'd been wasting. I vowed from that point forward to always exert my best effort—no matter the task or competition.

That point is when everything started to come together. The peace of mind I have gained in doing so has been invaluable. Nowadays, when I assume a role or partake in an endeavor, I am able to walk away knowing that I gave it my best shot. As a result, the toughest battle—the one within—has already been won. So, why worry? I encourage you to assess yourself and determine if you too have been meddling in mediocrity. If so, make a conscious decision to abort your approach to your mission, alter your course of action, and observe the abrupt change, both within yourself, as well as in your work performance.

Dr. Martin Luther King, Jr. emphasized this point when he stated: *"If a man is called to be a street sweeper, he should sweep streets even as a Michelangelo painted pictures, or Beethoven composed music or Shakespeare wrote poetry. He should sweep streets so well that all the hosts of heaven and earth will pause to say, 'Here lived a great street sweeper who did his job well.'"*

Imagine if you were leading an organization and everyone under your direction operated under this line of thinking—from the custodians up to the second in charge. Talk about a well-oiled machine! You'd have your entire department performing the white-glove test on everything they do. As everyone well knows, however, it all starts with the leader.

Fortunately, you are getting a head start as a young professional. Set. Go!

The Point Person

When I began my career in 2012 as a graduate assistant with the American Football Coaches Association (AFCA), I had no idea what buying in really entailed. As I settled in, Tai began assigning tasks that had value I did not immediately realize. It all just seemed like busy-work. Little did I know that he was strategically establishing buy-in.

One of the first things he had me do was type Coach Grant Teaff's Twenty-One Points, a transcription of Teaff's vision for the AFCA that he articulated when he took over the organization as its executive director in 1994. I completed the assignment fairly quickly and proceeded to inform Tai, assuming he would be impressed that it had not taken me very long. He then posed the question: "What did you think about it?"

I returned to my desk to read over the document more thoroughly so as to offer an informed opinion. What I initially thought would take about five minutes turned into an hour. After comparing what I typed up to what was in place around me, I was immediately awestruck. I double-checked the date of the publication, as well as my desk calendar, to ensure that it was indeed August and not April 1st.

Publication Year: 1994; Current Date: August 20, 2012. *Each of the twenty-one points Coach Teaff had proposed almost two decades earlier had come to fruition.*

It was then that I realized I was either working for a prophet or highly exceptional leader. (I'm convinced it's a combination of the two, given Coach Teaff's unquestioned faith.) This introduction to the organization resonated and immediately communicated that it was incumbent of me not to detract from the environment that had been created. As such, I was bought in. In fact, to this day, I still volunteer for the annual AFCA Convention every January. It is somewhat astonishing to think that all of this began as a simple assignment and follow-up question.

Jumping ahead to the 2013 AFCA Convention, I was determined to prove my worth. My preliminary work was all well and good, but Tai intimated that how I performed at the convention would ultimately communicate my value to the organization. I was initially assigned to work with Tai's operations team to ensure that everything ran smoothly from a logistics standpoint. Just as we were about to conduct our pre-convention meeting, however, Ms. Janet Robertson approached and shared the troubling news that Coach Teaff had fallen ill and was essentially bedridden. Though he was expected to bounce back soon, he would likely require an assistant throughout the convention.

After much discussion and apparent consternation, they settled on me. In every way possible, I am hard-pressed to effectively convey the gravity of this assignment. A then wide-eyed, 22-year-old graduate student from Grenada, Mississippi, was being tasked with escorting one of the most revered figures in all of college sports. Coach Teaff had been inducted into eight, count 'em EIGHT, halls of fame.

In contrast, you then have me. Mere weeks before the conference, it was brought to my attention that I was required to be in a suit anytime I was sporting an AFCA badge. Mind you, the last time that I'd worn a suit had been for Mother's Day during my senior year of high school. Flashback just six months earlier, when I was working at Walmart, and you would find my managers having a hard time getting me to wear the correct shades of blue and khaki. What a difference a year makes? Try 180 days!

Nonetheless, this situation was my opportunity to put my level of buy-in on full display, and I was not about to let it go to waste. Given Coach Teaff's platform, he was required to make countless appearances throughout the conference, often in various locations widespread throughout the building. The 2013 Convention was held at the Gaylord Opryland Resort in Nashville, Tennessee, essentially a city within a city. I don't recall going outside the resort that entire week.

With Coach's schedule in hand, I had a fellow staffer verify that it was in fact for one week's worth of engagements and not three. In some cases, he would need to attend multiple meetings in locations spread throughout the resort within the first 20 minutes of each starting. I knew that time would be of the essence, and that there would not be any to spare for going off in ill-advised directions.

As I mulled over all of this, the pre-convention meeting wore on until about 11:30 p.m. After adjourning, I ventured out to locate every room on Coach Teaff's schedule—making note of every escalator, pathway, service elevator, and shortcut known to man. I think I even found a trap door or two. I repeated this process nightly so that Coach Teaff could focus on advancing the AFCA's mission of educating football coaches. Because I had one job, it was to be performed at an optimal level. As a result, we didn't so much as even *look* in the wrong direction throughout the conference.

Consistent with Coach Teaff's servant leadership, he introduced me to everyone he encountered and allowed me to sit in on his high-profile meetings. In less than six months, I'd gone from stocking shelves to having conversations with prominent figures, such as Mack Brown (formerly the head football coach at the University of Texas) and Mark Emmert (the president of the NCAA).

Above and beyond those circumstances, what kept me going was the awareness that my job with Coach Teaff would affect the thousands of coaches and administrators in attendance. These same attendees would, in turn, regurgitate the AFCA's teachings to student-athletes and fellow administrators at their respective institutions. For a high school has-been like me, that is an incomparable cause to be a part of, even if no one else viewed the happenings the way I did.

Laying claim to small victories should be an integral component of your personal buy-in and motivation. It is a tactic to which I will subscribe, no matter what professional role I may hold or responsibility I may be assigned. Similarly, no matter your position or involvement, there will always be expectations for you to meet and, ideally, exceed. The gumption to excel arises out of a sense of personal accountability that is first cultivated by clearly defined expectations on the part of your leader.

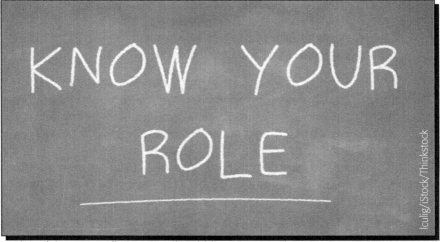

Laying claim to small victories should be an integral component of your personal buy-in and motivation.

The Blueprint – Leadership Perspective

Forward Management (© Tai M. Brown)

❏ **PHASE #1: CREATION**

3. Descriptive Expectations – *How will you evaluate your staff?* Now that you have made the hire, you'll need to explain the responsibilities of the position, and more importantly, define the standards of performance for how you expect the job to be done. Effectively doing these two things leaves no grey area when it comes time for staff evaluations because by doing so, you have essentially laid the foundation for organizational accountability. You'll find that after defining expectations and explaining responsibilities, people will do one of the following four things: 1). Do the job; 2). Excel at the job; 3). Choose not to do the job; or 4). Realize they don't have the ability to perform the job.

When standards and initiative are joined at the hip, it is hardly rivaled by any other dynamic. The leader is charged with setting the tone through Descriptive Expectations, but it is up to you to make the actual noise in harmonic fashion. Deliberate intent with this practice augments your drive to go above and beyond self-imposed limitations. Furthermore, buying-in in this sense does not subtract from your career capital. Rather, it makes a recurring deposit that will pay substantial dividends for years to come.

FOUNDATIONAL FOOTINGS

Buy Your Way In

I. Make a deliberate decision to hold yourself accountable for your thoughts, actions, and the service you provide to those you work for.

CHAPTER 2
Leggo My Ego

Feed the soul. Starve the ego.

—Adam Goldstein

It is easy to become enticed by the exorbitant salaries that some professionals earn these days, especially when growing up in a time where many of us seek instant gratification, somewhat like grits in the morning. It is not helpful to bore you with trite statements about how you probably will not make much money starting out or tales of the hardships that you are sure to face. Arguably, if you are following your passion, what does any of that matter?

What this chapter does offer you is advice on two "E" words that will bring your career to a halt faster than a thief in a bait car—ego and entitlement. The term "ego" has taken on an innately negative connotation over time, but it is really not as bad as some individuals might make it seem. The word "ego" is simply defined as a person's sense of self-esteem or self-importance. Hopefully, every aspiring professional possesses a healthy dose of this basic attribute. On the other hand, as you might imagine, an overbearing ego can be cancerous to your development as a rising professional.

You should be able to accept constructive criticism, as well as forthrightly admit when you are wrong. Otherwise, it will be difficult to sharpen or add tools to your toolbox. For example, there may be things you know how to do well, but that does not necessarily signify that you have mastery over that particular task. Likewise, a pretentious attitude will quickly alienate others and preclude you from learning a new craft or improving on an existing one.

In reality, there is usually a better way to do something. As such, it is in your best interests to be perceived as welcoming of new ideas and insight. Accordingly, you need to empower yourself to ask as many appropriate questions of your leaders and colleagues as feasible, especially in your early experiences. You will be surprised at what you didn't know you didn't know. Consider the consequences of that point for a moment.

You should approach every day in the likeness of a sponge. In other words, absorb every bit of non-confidential information you can around the workplace. Take a break from using your headphones and see if you can pick up something of value from high level conversations around the office. It can only serve to broaden your understanding of how your efforts fit into the bigger picture of your organization's purpose.

Tell Me What You Know

Upon entering the workforce, I considered myself to be openly welcoming of input and instruction. It was not until I learned of the variety of ego-based behavior that I realized some changes on my part were in order.

At some point, you will undoubtedly run across people who are good at what they do, are fully aware of it, and will constantly remind you of it in some form or fashion. If you hold such a perception about your higher-ups, you probably will not feel led to share your feedback—especially if they are stuck in their ways and unwilling to heed input. Thankfully, my first work experience under Tai was the complete opposite. I was given full autonomy over my assignments, and my feedback was taken into account without reservation. Not surprisingly, my early success naturally built confidence, and I began to think that the manner in which I went about arriving at solutions was best. Boy was I wrong.

Oftentimes, I would already have my mind made up and would not seek feedback on what I already thought to be valid. One day, it dawned on me that I needed to reevaluate how I went about carrying out assignments, regardless of my background knowledge or personal insight. It was the summer of 2013, and I was as busy as ever, mostly by my own doing. From summer courses to athletic performance coaching, not to mention my AFCA duties, I was all over the place.

In addition to those responsibilities, we were preparing for the Coaching School hosted by the Texas High School Coaches Association, the largest of its type in the country. It was customary for the AFCA to have a booth presence at the conference, among hundreds of other exhibitors. Our high school liaison, Johnny Tusa, had recently taken the athletic director job at Waco ISD, so we were an individual short. Because we were afforded a substantial footprint in the exhibit hall, we would require some outside assistance to fully staff the booth.

Tai asked me if I knew of any classmates with a vested interest in coaching football, someone who would benefit from the experience. My friend Brody Trahan was the first guy to come to mind. He had the pedigree and was actively pursuing a career in football coaching. The only caveat was that he was still playing linebacker for the Baylor football team, and summer workouts were in full swing. I knew full well because I was rising at 4:15 a.m., four days a week, to coach them.

Armed with knowledge of the attendance polices and punishments for absences, I informed Tai that Brody likely would not be able to commit. The last thing I wanted to do was create a conflict of interest dilemma for a friend of mine, so I decided not to mention the opportunity to Brody at all. Over the next few weeks, Tai asked me time and time again about Brody's interest in working the Coaching School, as the event was fast approaching. Each time, I provided him with my first-hand knowledge of the situation, citing the likelihood of Brody being able to participate as pretty slim. After all, I saw the guy working his tail off every day and did not want him to fall behind on the depth chart.

Eventually, there came a critical point at which we had to find *someone* to fulfill our staffing needs. Once again, Tai asked me about Brody's status. I gave him the same generic answer that I had been offering over the past few weeks, but it didn't quite suffice this time. I feel that I am pretty good at reading people, so let's just say I felt it necessary for me to get an answer directly from Brody before sharing any more of my "expert" advice.

You can guess what happened next. I gauged Brody's interest, and as expected, he was ecstatic about the opportunity to get a head start on his dream career path. When I brought up the summer workouts caveat and how the Coaching School may conflict with the final week of workouts, he said he would check with his assigned performance coach.

Lo and behold, Brody found out that the team's workouts were being curtailed the latter part of the week in question and that he would be available to work the Coaching School. Subsequently, I shared this development with Tai. Instead of him rubbing it in my face like he should have, he was just glad to have someone on board. He knew that I was able to reasonably assess situations in which I found myself. Therefore, he left it up to me to figure out where I had gone wrong from the outset.

It was after I'd analyzed the situation from start to finish that I sat down to offer my apologies for not following directions from the beginning. He did not fault me in the slightest. Instead, he leveled with me and conveyed how multi-faceted ego-based behavior could be and its crippling effects. The key takeaway was that when we get in our own way, we often find ourselves inadvertently in the way of others and the bigger picture.

This experience reminds me of a story longtime athletics devotee Dutch Baughman often shares at speaking engagements. He had a similar experience when he was an assistant coach under the legendary Woody Hayes at The Ohio State University. In a nutshell, Coach Hayes had instructed young Baughman to scout the Buckeyes' opponent for the upcoming week. As Baughman tells it, he recalls preparing this great report and speaks of how he was primed to present it to Coach Hayes at a moment's notice. After all, this was his chance to prove himself to the head coach.

He and Coach Hayes eventually carved out some time to discuss the report, and Baughman discloses that he began his discourse with, "Well coach, I think…" Hayes stopped him in his tracks and replied, "Dutchman, don't tell me what you think. Tell me what you know." Lesson learned. Baughman went on to become an athletic director at multiple Division 1 institutions and later served as executive director of the Division 1-A Athletic Directors' Association by the way.

I know that much.

The second "E" word is entitlement. This mindset is by far the most polarizing characteristic young professionals are believed to carry in the modern workforce. The definition of entitlement reads as the belief that one inherently deserves privileges or special treatment. Call me crazy, but a persona of this nature may not go over too well with your leader.

It is not as though this all-too-common characteristic is purposeful. In fact, too many individuals fail to even realize that they exude this type of 'tude. Arguably, such a demeanor is merely an unintended consequence of our increased consumption of mass media and its augmenting effects on our ambition. That factor is not a justifiable excuse, however. While ambition is not a crime in itself, entitled ambition will land you a career sentence quick, fast, and in a hurry.

For years, people may have told you how great you are and how bright your future is—feedback, all factors considered, is quite alright. In fact, everyone needs encouragement and reassurance every now and again. In your haste to fulfill such prophecies, however, you could quickly lose touch with what it takes to turn your potential into prosperity. It requires solidifying your foundation brick by brick with any and every job you are assigned, and sometimes even the ones you aren't.

For those individuals who are—or soon will be—partaking in what you may deem menial tasks, know this: You are not doing anything someone before you hasn't done. In fact, with technological advances, you probably have it far easier than your leaders did when they were in your position. Again, the most important thing for you to do is to show you are ready and willing to do whatever, whenever. This demonstrated inclination is the only way to establish credibility in the minds of those people who are pulling the strings and making calls on your behalf.

The Blueprint – Leadership Perspective

Forward Management (© Tai M. Brown)

❏ **PHASE #1: CREATION**

4. Dutiful Duties – *Does your staff know why each job is important?* The big picture is made up of many small pictures, therefore, extraordinary execution on the small scale allows for exceptional execution on the large scale. If you have explained how everything ties to the purpose, then you should be able to explain how each assignment—whether large or small—has a role in successfully fulfilling that purpose.

You never know how, when, or where your work will be used, so always execute assignments at a high level (there goes that phrase again). Leading up to the 2014 AFCA Convention, when interest in the college football concussion issue was at its height, I recall conducting research for Coach Teaff about the safety initiatives AFCA had implemented in the past. I was aware Coach Teaff would be using it, but imagine how I felt when then AFCA president and former University of Texas football coach Mack Brown randomly asked for a copy to read at a general session with over 3,000 attendees. Good thing I brought my A-game!

That experience taught me there should never be a dilemma when it comes to giving a first-class effort, no matter your level of responsibility. Imagine the consistency in your quality of work if you went about every assignment as if the CEO was going to depend solely on what you submit, absent the benefit of any background knowledge.

If the aforementioned does not light a fire under you, who knows what will? The importance of protecting the head coach will be discussed in a later chapter. In the grand scheme of things, however, it all boils down to doing the best job possible with what has already been entrusted to you. Absent such focus, a counterproductive effect may result and handicap all of the individuals who have stake in a particular initiative. In addition, no matter how insurmountable they may seem, your personal performance standards should always be higher than those that have been laid out for you.

If subjective performance evaluations are the only means by which you assess your competency, your standards are far too low. What if you walked into that meeting having already conducted a performance audit on yourself? It may not be typed out, but you should definitely have a mental report on file. No surprises should arise from performance assessments—only confirmation of what you already know to be true— whether superlative or sub-par.

The unheralded tasks are often what most invigorate your drive, even though they will not remain as your primary responsibilities for the rest of your career. On the other hand, you should never get above them. Taking on such responsibilities makes you respect the hard work that goes into accomplishing high-level goals, and if you remain cognizant of them, it will enhance your ability to lead those individuals who will one day report to you.

This aptitude will be due, in part, to your genuine ability to both relate to what your reports are doing, as well as actively convey how their contribution fits into the bigger picture. This picture should no longer be as blurry to you as it once was, when you were in their position. It will then be incumbent on you, as a leader, to bring that image into focus and skew the inverse relationship between buying-in and entitlement in your favor.

Hab1ts = One thing, one percent better, one day at a time.

More often than not, the unconventional ideas and strategies that people come up with are what separate them from the pack. Such ingenuity usually comes about as a direct result of placing strong emphasis on otherwise insignificant tasks and applying an intricate understanding of how processes function from a grassroots level. This stage is where the seeds of servant-leadership are sown and fittingly fertilized, ultimately producing a rich harvest. A little food for thought for you down the road.

As you journey to reach your destination, it may feel as though you are sometimes walking barefoot on a gravel path. This feeling is not uncommon for young professionals. As such, if you need to pat yourself on the back every now and again, then go right ahead. I have found that successfully completing lesser assignments in the early stages is paramount to building your level of confidence for more significant responsibilities as they come along.

All in all, the great don't just become great instantaneously. What they have known to be true for quite some time has just been a tactical, timed-release that everyone else will eventually come to realize.

FOUNDATIONAL FOOTINGS

Leggo My Ego

II. Until you know that you don't always know, you will not know what you are capable of knowing and, thus, accomplishing.

CHAPTER 3
Transition: Be Where You Are

When starting with a new organization, you will enter with non-traditional concepts and ideas from previous experiences. In this scenario, your insight as a new employee—someone who has yet to even locate the restrooms—can prove invaluable. You have the platform to make an immediate impact, based solely on your "ignorance" of the established systems and protocols. This concept is referred to as "invaluable ignorance."

Utilize this "ignorance" as a reservoir of professional capital to immediately begin investing into your organization, while getting acclimated to the new setting. This phase of the onboarding process comes complete with buffers that will allow and thereby empower you to begin sharing your input against minimal resistance. At this point, you are still the new guy. You don't know any better. Or do you?

You will not know until you explore your offerings. As you unearth your talents, understand you will likely make a few mistakes early on. This situation is natural for new hires, so embrace it. The point of this phase is to decide how you will react to and channel the lessons learned from these early mistakes to enhance your overall work performance moving forward. Have you ever heard of a make-up call by a referee?

You can apply this concept to your job, absent the heckling from crazed fans. In other words, although you may have fallen short on a given task, you should seek to blow everyone away with your follow-up effort. This forward thinking attitude serves as a source of motivation and propagates momentum for future projects to come.

Your line of thinking will segue from the self-serving, "What am I doing?" to the more altruistic, "What am I doing to *make this better?*" General George S. Patton is credited with saying, "If everyone is thinking alike, then someone isn't thinking." As such, you should begin generating all the input you can before your "new guy window" closes, and your vision starts to become myopic.

In doing so, you will learn more about the company and be equipped to offer greater insight moving forward. Even if you get wind of something that most individuals may regard as a dead-end, you should press forward in your quest to debunk systematic lines of thinking. You may just stumble upon a groundbreaking improvement for the betterment of the entire unit. At that point, you go from rogue to rock star.

As long as your intentions are firmly rooted in advancing your organization's purpose, there is nothing wrong with going out on a limb. Such ventures help to inform you early on as to what type of leadership you are operating under. Was your leader receptive to the ideas you shared? Did he at least try to implement some of your input on a given project?

The Blueprint – Leadership Perspective

Forward Management (© Tai M. Brown)

❏ **PHASE #2: CULTIVATION**

6. Responsive Feedback – *People want to know their input is heard and potentially useful.* Encourage input from your staff. By doing so, they feel they have a say in the project you are building. Help them help you by doing the following: 1). Listen to their ideas; 2). Provide feedback on their ideas; 3). Determine if their ideas can be implemented; and 4). If one of them can be implemented, proceed to implement it. Allowing your employees to have input in important decisions will lead them to further embrace the company culture.

While you should always intake as much information as possible, you should be prudent in determining the appropriate settings and methods by which to share your feedback, if at all. Sometimes, great value exists in keeping pensively mum until you have a firm grasp on the lay of the land.

One well-respected leader states that there are two common pitfalls employees at any level should steer clear of: (1) offering suggestions for organizational efficiency without first having your responsibilities taken care of; and (2) bringing forth any issues, without any semblance of thought or rationale for potential solutions. Drawback #1 is pretty straightforward: do your job. Your lackluster performance may very well be the kink in the system, but because you are too busy concerning yourself with other happenings, you remain oblivious and look to place blame elsewhere. Mirror, mirror on the wall.

With regard to peril #2, your solution does not necessarily have to be the best one, but you can further communicate your value and care for the organization by at least *proposing* methods by which to resolve a given issue. In any case, how your input is received and whether it is implemented or not is out of your control.

Of the vast wealth of knowledge often handed down through the ranks, one of the most common pieces of advice proffered to young professionals is: Be where you are. I recall my first time hearing this phrase and thinking it was the most redundant thing I had ever heard. I mean, where else could I possibly be other than where I am? I must admit, though, considering the standing of the professional I first heard it from, I was tempted to reply, "How about you just let me be where *you* are, and we call it even?" Ah, if only it were that simple, right?

I later learned the significant value hidden in that quartet of words and found why it was, in fact, the first piece of advice I was ever given. Absent my first adhering to that counsel, every bit of practical advice to follow would have been rendered useless. Being where you are essentially means to be subsumed with the opportunity at hand and focused solely on advancing the responsibilities and expectations that have already been entrusted to you. This feat can only be accomplished by doing your part at the highest level possible, without allowing external distractions to creep in. As was discussed previously, you must first get bought in above all else.

Adopt the mindset that what you are doing in your current role is essentially what is keeping the earth rotating on its axis. Assume a mentality that leads you to believe that any lackluster work performance or fixation with an organization other than your own will ultimately lead to the apocalypse. Okay, maybe it's not *that* serious, but it's pretty close.

People who allow external influences to determine their level of drive become reactive in nature. As a result, they relinquish all power to outside forces, leaving them at a competitive disadvantage before the lights even come on. At this juncture, the focus becomes centered on reacting to situations, rather than leading the charge.

You also have individuals who are, first and foremost, competing against themselves—the most formidable of possible opponents. These individuals consistently produce at the same rate and level, regardless of the given circumstances and without having to be importuned. After all, what you do when no one is looking is what truly defines who you are.

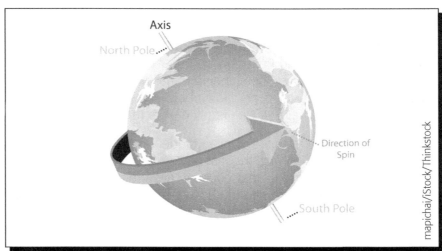

Adopt the mindset that what you are doing in your current role is essentially what is keeping the earth rotating on its axis.

This factor directly correlates with your buy-in as a young professional. Once you have primed your mentality, small jobs become far easier to take on as you come to realize that they are crucial to satisfying the organization's overarching goals. You begin to understand that your contribution is indispensable and thus take pride in making it count. If you do not aspire to leave your mark wherever you are, you should prepare to be mentioned in the same breath as everyone who came before you. In which case, you then become average. You know, mediocre. Ordinary.

The importance of taking pride in what you do can neither be overstated nor taken for granted. It is the line of demarcation that separates you from everyone else, no matter what gaps in experience or skillsets may exist. It aligns with the saying of, "Hard work beats talent." Talent can be developed, but work ethic cannot be taught. Your work ethic is ingrained in your competitive appetite and can only be satiated by operating at a high level.

The Blueprint – Leadership Perspective

Forward Management (© Tai M. Brown)

❑ **PHASE #2: CULTIVATION**

7. Productive Motivation Cycle – *Productivity breeds motivation.* Create frequent and consistent evaluation tools for measuring productivity so your staff can see how their accomplishments help to fulfill the purpose. When people see positive results from their efforts, they are motivated to continue producing those results. Also, if you have successfully shown how fulfilling the purpose will help them in their personal and professional development, they will then be motivated by an even stronger stimulant—their own success.

In fact, accounting for a few experiential differences, most résumés are essentially the same these days. What gets your illustrious piece of paper out of the big stack and into the smaller one is the amount of care your references perceive about you while under their direction. A given reference may share *what* you did while working for him as a formality, but the manner in which he describes *how* you went about doing it will ultimately prove to be the difference-maker in your consideration.

Therein showcases the stark distinction between buying-in and being where you are, as opposed to merely participating. The peaking upside to operating with a bought in attitude is exhibiting a manner of doing things that etch far deeper than anything you could ever document on your résumé. Such actions inscribe your intent, describe your determination, and subscribe to your success. This level of drive is what ultimately gets you from where you are to where you want to be.

FOUNDATIONAL FOOTINGS

Be Where You Are

III. Aspire to make your contribution indispensable.

FOUNDATIONAL FOOTINGS

Part I: The Lay of the Land

Buy Your Way In

I. Make a deliberate decision to hold yourself accountable for your thoughts, actions, and the service you provide to those you work for.

Leggo My Ego

II. Until you know that you don't always know, you will not know what you are capable of knowing and, thus, accomplishing.

Be Where You Are

III. Aspire to make your contribution indispensable.

PART II
Cultivating Your
Career Field

At this point, you should be well-trained enough to go 12 rounds against yourself and emerge victorious. Nevertheless, there is always the threat of the outside competition that you will be up against as you pursue your goals. The lessons in part I were directed primarily at shaping your mentality. In contrast, in part II, it is now time to get a little more practical in preparation for the external opposition you are sure to face. The following questions can be employed as checks and balances to both gauge and guide your career progression:

- Have you contributed to the body of knowledge in any way?

- Is anyone soliciting advice from you on how to do their job better?

- Have you been #1 in the nation in your *current* role?

Although no definitive method exists for determining your actual ranking, that is no excuse. If you are honest with yourself and knowledgeable of what your counterparts are doing around the industry, you should be able to extrapolate some fairly trustworthy data and address these questions head-on. On one hand, these self-check probes can be quite humbling. On the other hand, at the same time, they can also be equally motivational. They were not posed to discourage you, but rather to serve as a reminder that your best days are, in fact, ahead of you and that there is still much work to be done. Be where you are, approach your current opportunity with unparalleled vigor, and set the bar out of reach.

CHAPTER 4
Hunter-Gatherers

*Give a man a fish and you feed him
for a day; teach a man how to fish
and you feed him for a lifetime.*

—Chinese proverb

History offers a real-life example of operating successfully in your role against external competition. The early hunter-gatherer civilizations competed against nature—the ultimate external competition—to lead successful lives. They succeeded in these pursuits by gathering specific resources, garnering knowledge of what to do with these resources, and working closely with each other to increase their status.

Cross-cultural historical findings describe hunter-gatherers as those individuals who were less prone to resource unpredictability, famines, and food shortages due to their tenacious attitude toward securing resources. This factor was due in part to the fact they harvested not only what was available around them, but they also focused on gathering specific products and combining them with other secondary resources.

Given that hunters-gatherers were the original sportsmen, this chapter is aptly titled to pay homage to those individuals who paved the way. Hunter-gatherers typically moved about in small bands, or groups of people, in their quests. Each band was known across a wide area, because all residents of a particular region were typically tied to one another through a large network of kinship and reciprocity. Hunter-gatherers were also revered for their distinct ability to acquire and use their wealth of knowledge to reach new heights.

Though the means by which people obtain essentials have evolved considerably since this primitive era, the strategies have not been altered. In other words, the players change, but the game remains the same. As such, young up-and-comers are constantly on the hunt for resources to help satiate their ambitions. While a plethora of information is literally at our fingertips these days, there is no substitute for learning directly from experienced practitioners.

In your quest to become the consummate professional, you will require resources of your own. One of the more useful tools in this regard is the informational interview, or sponging. These brain-picking sessions serve to add practicality to the base of knowledge you have acquired from completing coursework, among other sources. In a nutshell, if you are the smartest person in your network, it is time to channel your inner hunter-gatherer.

Because people in general love talking about themselves, you should expect a high success rate when soliciting informational interviews. Prior to the interview, you will want to do your background research and avoid asking questions that can be answered with a simple "yes" or "no." Furthermore, you should refrain from asking questions Google could answer with a few quick key strokes. It's annoying.

Many professionals remember when they were in your shoes and genuinely want to help you. It has been said that a person's success can only be measured by how many other people they help become successful. As such, the obvious question is why not help others help you? The earlier you begin planting seeds in the minds of prominent professionals, the quicker and richer your harvest will be.

The sheer luxury of being a wide-eyed recent graduate or entry-leveler is the fact you have the freedom to explore as many different facets of the business as you like without reproach. Few people would expect you to declare a distinct path at this point in your career. There are too many nuances to evaluate. It is like having the opening break in a billiards game and knocking in both a striped and solid-colored ball. You would not commit to playing one or the other without first surveying the landscape of the pool table and the ball displacement.

Since you are competing to win the game, you are expected to develop a strategy to do so. The same approach applies to beginning your career; your options are wide open.

When surveying the landscape of your chosen field of endeavor and the displacement of the job openings in that field, you should be sure to approach this process strategically. For example, if you come across a job posting that you are not yet qualified for, but would like to secure that position or one like it in the future, you should print out the job description and use it as a model for your career path. It will provide straightforward bullet points in areas in which you need to gain experience, as well as highlight skills that you may need to improve upon. Once the position is filled, the posting will be taken down—leaving you ambulating aimlessly in pursuit of something for which you no longer know the pertinent qualifications. Take advantage of every resource available to you, given that there is value to be discovered in everything. The point you need to remember is that it is essential that you remain focused on the process, no matter what stage of it you may be in.

Duncan Smith/Photodisc/Thinkstock

It has been said that a person's success can only be measured by how many other people they help become successful.

Widen Your Stance

"The workforce is competitive." Hmm...now where have I heard that before? The first time I heard that statement, I longed for the litany of ways to gain a competitive advantage. What I found is that a person must first humbly adopt the mindset that he is a beast and up for any challenge...and *then* some. Grrrrr.

Okay, let's discuss less barbarian strategies by which you may position yourself favorably. First of all, although you do not have to master every skillset under the sun to be successful, it is best that you have a working knowledge of as many facets of the business as possible.

Seldom does an individual-in-charge know how to do every one of the jobs of the people who report to him. On the other hand, he does know how to get the best out of them. This attribute requires a great deal of political skill, most notably social astuteness with respect to being able to assess situations and adapt to various personalities with tailored motivational tactics. Though you may not be supervising anyone just yet, the same methodology applies for when you are working laterally with coworkers.

The key point is that you need to be strategic in determining best practices for not only achieving objectives without alienating your colleagues, but also in coalition-building in the midst of your endeavors. Because this dynamic can be tricky, you should proceed with caution. Arguably, few people like being told what to do, especially by someone at the same perceived occupational level as they are. Thus, all factors considered, your delivery of a given message is just as important, if not more, than the actual content of that message.

Imagine if you and another person were side-shuffling across a narrow platform at a high elevation, and both of you were required to move simultaneously to counterbalance the other's weight. Although a fully collaborative effort, someone still has to lead the effort, while remaining mindful that the person next to them is required to successfully traverse the platform. The last thing you want to do is anger your counterpart through terse communication, causing that individual to take a misstep that will ultimately lead to your collective demise.

Conceivably, you are basically following this example in working with your counterparts on important assignments.

Basic biomechanics denote that the narrower your anatomical stance, the more confined your base of support. As such, your physical stability will be compromised. No sport actions requiring physical activity may be performed optimally with a confined base of support. Imagine if you were attempting to defend a basketball player with your feet side by side. You might as well prepare to commit a hard foul, because there is no way you would be able to stay in front of him. In another hypothetical situation, if you were batting in a baseball game, can you imagine how difficult it would be to get the bat around with your ankles nearly touching?

These examples are analogous to the difficulties you face with an inadequate base of human support. As such, workplace relationships should be envisioned as a unified body, with you figuratively serving as the torso and your colleagues as its extremities. Accordingly, you should be proactive in widening your base of supportive individuals in the workplace. In that regard, you should begin to identify people who would not warrant you taking a sneak peek before performing a trust fall to ensure they are still behind you. The focus should be on those folks that you know will be there to catch and uplift you when you teeter.

Otherwise, as the examples suggest, it is going to be extremely difficult to accomplish anything. Would you prefer to work with someone who is cooperating because they have to, or rather someone who is more concerned with your well-being as a rising professional? I'll take what's behind the second door.

Although in-game adjustments in sport are commonplace, any coach will tell you that he would prefer to be fully prepared at the start of the contest, rather than risk falling behind early and being forced to react. The same factor applies to workplace relationships. You should seek to cultivate meaningful associations with other individuals, even when there is nothing at stake. The peace of mind you gain from knowing your peers are rooting for you can serve to help boost your confidence when it is time to step up to the plate and execute.

You should be proactive in widening your base of supportive individuals in the workplace.

Building relationships with people working in organizations outside of your direct practice is also of paramount importance. This feat may be accomplished by volunteering your most precious commodity—your time. In doing so, because you have no hidden agenda or imminent gain to be realized, you are able to form a deep sense of trust. As a result, you become an asset.

In similar manner, you don't become important to others until what's important to them becomes important to you. You never know what tips you may pick up to increase the efficacy and quality of your work. Thus, voluntarily immersing yourself in someone else's fire is sometimes the best way to get cooking.

There is often a number of ways to reach a common goal, but you will never know how your method stacks up, if you neglect to observe or take instruction from someone who may go about a similar task differently. For example, you may drive a Corvette, and someone else may own a Prius, but that does not mean that the other individual doesn't know how to get somewhere faster than you via an alternate route.

Dutch Baughman counsels that an individual should determine where the duties of his job intersect with those of employees in other departments within the company. By collaboratively detecting such critical points, you may begin streamlining important processes to ease each other's workload. This initiative works two-fold, given that you now have an opportunity to pick a fellow staffer's brain and possibly acquire new skills to add to your arsenal in the process. There is no speed limit in the pursuit of excellence. The path is jagged enough as is without the added worry of your progress being slowed by a lack of perspective.

Furthermore, your work life will have far more meaning if you chase potential over pay. At some point, the pay will come as you seek to reach your potential. On the other hand, the reverse of that line of thought does not apply. Your goal should be to become seemingly indispensable. Once that becomes a trend as you rise through the ranks, guess what begins to happen? Your reputation begins to precede you, and your value increases. The opportunities will now begin to find YOU. Finally, you may find it apropos to change your homepage from that job board website. Back to Google you go!

Design Your Destiny

As a graduate student, I interned under Candice Walls, a vibrant young woman, who serves as an athletic performance coach. One day, we were discussing her journey to her current position and how she was able to rise through the ranks so rapidly. As part of our conversation, I asked her what the difference was, and she offered the same advice that is being shared in this chapter.

Her response was that, early in her career, she went outside the scope of what a normal job description for a performance coach would call for and learned graphic design. This unique skill served to separate her from the pack and ultimately led to her rapid ascension. Nowadays, weekly messages complete with sublime graphics don every monitor in the weight facility and serve as the cornerstone of the program's sport psychology initiative. Candice added value that the department didn't even know it needed, until the full extent and impact of her skillset was presented to the leadership.

As the late Steve Jobs once said, "People don't know what they want until we show them."

Indeed, Mr. Jobs. Indeed.

FOUNDATIONAL FOOTINGS

Hunter-Gatherers

IV. Seek out resources that help build your career capital.

CHAPTER 5
Protecting the Head Coach

Watch the throne.

Have you ever met someone so adept at their job that you could not imagine that person working for someone else? If you haven't, at some point in your life, you will. This caliber of professional is definitely out there. Aside from their outstanding networks, I have often wondered what set them apart from others vying for their positions.

We could go back and forth on the "who you know" mantra until the cows come home, but let's face it…some people are just darn *good*. In speaking with nationally recognized coaches and administrators about this issue, I have posed the same question to each of them, and the essence of their respective answers has been the same across the board.

First and foremost, make your leader look good by ensuring that he is not grossly affected by any unforeseen circumstances. Handle what you can handle, but be sure to keep your leader apprised of your actions. Great leaders boast a collection of quick-fix solutions that would take many of us a series of steps to determine.

Similarly, there is nothing wrong with conducting some mental management of your own as a young professional. For example, when fires above your rank need to be extinguished, consider how you would potentially douse them. Be honest, would you have gotten burned? More often than not, your solution will not be able to stand toe-to-toe with the one your higher-ups implemented. Other times, it may be just as good or an even better alternative. In either case, you have gained a new perspective.

Take the initiative to ensure the success of not only your leader, but your team members as well. Your team's success and preparedness will reflect the quality of leadership in the organization. Even if you are not directly credited with a specific feat, the team you represent will be held in high regard. Thus, your first goal is to try to become *associated* with sustained, high performance before attempting to blaze your own trail.

Ask yourself; what warrants your consideration for extra benefits, aside from how long you have been with the company? If you wish to be considered for salary increases and advancement, you must provide your leader with clear rationale for considering you for such perks. This feat is best accomplished by first protecting the foreman of your fortress.

The Blueprint – Leadership Perspective

Forward Management (© Tai M. Brown)

❑ PHASE #3: AFFIRMATION

(Affirm your staff as they have proven to be assets to you and your organization.)

8. Employee Recognition – *People want to feel valued.* If your staff has excelled at the job you have defined for them, exceeded the expectations you have laid out for them, provided valuable input on projects, and proven to be a productive asset, then you should recognize their contribution to the fulfillment of the purpose. Recognizing your staff as part of the reason for the team's success helps to foster a productive and enterprising culture they will embrace as a significant milestone in their career.

A growing trend among astute employers has been to contact individuals you may have worked with who are not, I repeat NOT, on your list of references. This means you have to be on your A-game at all times, as opposed to only in the presence of the high-profile individuals you plan to list as references. It is a given that the people you listed will vouch for you. What about those leaders you failed to list from past jobs? Please know that if it's on your résumé, it is fair game.

Tai employed this approach with respect to my candidacy for the single AFCA graduate assistantship opening that came available in 2012. Before electing to try my hand at the administrative side of sport management, I was exclusively pursuing a career in strength and conditioning. The change of heart occurred midway through my strength and conditioning internship as a senior at Ole Miss. To a degree, a sense of apathy set into my life. Nevertheless, I remained steadfast in honoring my commitment to Ole Miss and ensured that there was no dip in my performance for the remainder of the internship.

In crafting my résumé, I was sure to include my strength and conditioning background, since it was the only sport-related experience that I'd garnered up to that point. On the other hand, for no reason other than being naïve, I neglected to list my former program director, Coach John Simmons, as a reference. Subsequently, I later learned that Tai had identified the omission and elected to reach out to Coach Simmons.

As Tai relays the story, Coach Simmons implied he was, in fact, aware of my shift in interest, but reassured Tai that I remained committed to the program and continued to do everything asked of me and more. Had I not maintained the level of performance I'd built my infantile profile around, the exchange between Tai and Coach Simmons could have very well worked against me.

Though I am not privy to what exactly transpired during the call between Tai and Coach Simmons, I am of the impression that it followed one of the following two scenarios:

> *A prospective employer calls someone on your reference list to inquire about your work ethic.*
>
> - *Response #1 (Your name here) was a good worker. He did everything we asked of him.*
>
> - *Response #2: (Your name here) was an outstanding employee. He went above and beyond what we asked of him without prompting.*

In my case, some form of the latter response is what I'd like to believe was transmitted on my behalf, and it made all the difference. Barring the addition of a few inconsequential words, neither potential response is very complex, albeit they communicate vastly different messages. If you really desired a particular position, in which response would you rather have your name inserted? Without question, response #2 is far superior to the former. With that in mind, how do you go about ensuring your name is inserted into the latter option?

As was discussed in the first chapter, buying in is imperative. In addition, you need to have the ability to "put out fires" and "see around corners," whenever possible. Your leader should never be blindsided by anything remotely detectable. As someone he brought on to help keep everything running smoothly, you are the first line of defense for potential intrusion or interruption of departmental homeostasis. Having the foresight to identify problems and potential solutions is a great way to convey competency to your leader and, as a result, to subsequently be trusted with greater responsibilities.

Micromanaging is one thing we all detest. It makes you question why you were even hired in the first place. This over-your-shoulder method is usually grounded in one of two things. Either your leader has an incurable case of micromanager mania, or maybe you have yet to build up enough trust to overcome his reservations. If it proves to be a case of the latter, this situation is your cue to take your production to the next level.

In doing so, a good rule-of-thumb is to always be prepared to communicate the rationale for why you may have taken initiative without your leader's input. Even if it does not exactly align with what your leader had in mind, at least he is made aware that your wheels are turning. He recognizes that you are seeking to make his job easier through actionable buy-in. Your leader will appreciate the fact that you're taking care of things he should not have to worry about. The question arises whether you will eventually reach a point in your career, when someone does the same for you. So, why not practice good medicine?

Yes, Allen Iverson, we're talking about practice.

Reflect & React

The end of the 2013 AFCA Convention was drawing near, and Coach Teaff appeared to be completely sold on the attention to detail and efficiency I had exhibited throughout the week. Accordingly, he trusted me with something that is very near and dear to his heart. At every convention, Coach Teaff carves out time in his schedule to celebrate a standout student from his high school alma mater, Snyder High School, in Snyder, Texas. He requires a minimum of five minutes be earmarked for this event. Even if we are running behind schedule, cutting this presentation is not an option.

More often than not, the honoree is unable to make it to the convention to accept the award in person. As a result, Coach Teaff has the presentation filmed in a forum of more than 4,000 coaches, who stand and applaud for almost two whole minutes. Afterward, the presentation is copied to DVD, and sent to Snyder High School. This scenario was, in fact, the case during the 2013 Convention. Later that day, as we were finishing up the day's engagements, Coach Teaff handed me the DVD of the presentation and asked that I make sure it was overnighted to Snyder High School for their banquet the following day. I assured him that I would take care of it, even though I was not privy to how our FedEx account was set up at the Gaylord Opryland Resort. That was none of his concern, however. He gave me a job to do, and it needed to be taken care of by any means necessary.

Initially, I tried to ship it on my own, but because my name was not on the list of approved staff members to mail packages, I was unsuccessful. As I headed back to our main office to figure out how to take care of it, I ran into Tai. I informed him of what Coach Teaff asked me to do and the hurdle that I'd run into trying to complete it. Tai fully understood the importance of getting the DVD mailed, given that he'd been in charge of handling the task for years prior. He said he would take care of it, so I counted it as done.

We were on the staff bus later that evening headed to the airport, both of us dog-tired from sleeping four hours or less over the previous five days. Both of our foreheads were buried into the seatbacks in front of us, and I was reflecting on the convention when it hit me. I asked

Tai if he remembered to overnight that DVD to Snyder High School. His head jerked so quickly that I was sure he had experienced whiplash. He gave me that uh-oh look.

Sparing the minutiae of details, this situation exemplifies the value of reflecting on your day or week and ensuring the protection of the head coach. Although Tai assured me he would handle it, and did ultimately, it began as MY responsibility. My responsibility was to see it through, despite the fact that I utilized his assistance. Had I not exhibited a high degree of care, Coach Teaff would have been embarrassed, and I would have squandered the remarkable credibility that I'd built up over the past few days. Furthermore, Tai would have felt terrible, as my proxy trustee for the assignment.

I cannot count the number of times that both of these gentlemen have helped me personally and professionally. Accordingly, I had to make sure that both individuals were adequately shielded. As you will learn in Chapter 7, Jersey Swap, if you want someone of influence to put his jersey on your back, you first have to show you have his backsides covered. If Coach Teaff is reading this, it will be his first time learning of how everything transpired, and rightfully so. He is the head coach. He only needed to be reassured that the assignment had been taken care of and that he had been protected.

FOUNDATIONAL FOOTINGS

Protecting the Head Coach

V. Allow your leader to excel by being excellent.

CHAPTER 6
Transition: Branding & Blossoming

Be more concerned with your character than your reputation, because your character is what you really are, while your reputation is merely what others think you are.

—John Wooden

Unlike washable tattoos, your brand never washes away. As University of Mississippi athletic director Ross Bjork once informed me, the logo never comes off. In his case, he is still the athletic director, whether he is shopping at Walmart or hosting an event for major donors. Bjork's advice is not to be taken out of context, however. Citing one of Colin Powell's remarkable leadership lessons, "Never let your ego get so close to your position that when your position goes, your ego goes with it."

Positions are like opinions. Depending on who offers them, some will appear more viable than others, but none of them really matter at the end of the day. Just think, if you surrendered your job post and every material possession you owned, what would you still have? Your name…as well as what people attribute to it when they hear it. The process of developing, managing, and protecting your brand is not to be taken lightly.

Brand Development

Become a sponge. The key point to remember is that you should take something away from the qualities of everyone you come in contact with—both good and bad. You need to recall how each person made you feel, so you can retain the most endearing qualities and eschew the less favorable ones. Furthermore, you should attend as many conferences and professional development opportunities as possible to absorb all you can.

Brand Management

You must objectively determine the current stature of your brand and what heights you desire it to reach in the future. As you begin your career, your brand management should be predicated on your willingness to do anything and everything to prosper your organization. The small details will not go unnoticed; someone is always watching. Is the outside perception of your brand consistent with how you think you are portraying it? Step behind the two-way mirror and have a look for yourself.

Brand Protection

Your brand must be regarded as a sacred commodity that you work assiduously to safeguard. Attacks may arise, both seen and unseen, that could serve to compromise your brand. Whether it is your social media activity or the company you keep, it all reflects back to you. Hiding behind screennames or handles will not mask any distorted images you have created for yourself. Conversely, the person you are when no one is watching shall determine the professional you will become.

Furthermore, your brand will precede, position, and protect you, as the following notes:

- *Precede:* As you prepare to sit for a job interview, your brand does not meet you there—it beats you there. Make sure it sets an atmosphere conducive to the outcome you are seeking.

- *Position:* Your interviewing skills and résumé components carry little weight in comparison to your brand. It alone could prove to be the ultimate determinant of whether or not you secure an opportunity.

- *Protect:* In light of your track record, people are cognizant of what you will and will not stand for.

Your brand, then, by its very nature, becomes your armor. Any chink in this armor exposes your brand to the elements of your field and allows for it to be exploited by external competition. It is best to ensure there is no grey area or disconnect in the positive manner you perceive yourself with regard to the perspectives of others.

The following quote by the prolific writer and blogger Jay Danzie helps put the importance of your brand in perspective: "Your smile is your logo, your personality is your business card, and how you leave others feeling after having an experience with you becomes your trademark." This trademarked feeling, as described by Danzie, refers to the seeds you plant in the hearts and minds of those with whom you connect. Such seeds, if nurtured, are sure to develop into budding relationships and bear fruit for a rich harvest—as you will see unfold in Part III of this book.

The cultivation process is one that is often taken for granted, as if planting seeds and failing to water them is conducive to growth. Absent consistent and genuine care for your deposits, the roots essential to strengthening your foothold will never materialize. Furthermore, if you have ever uprooted a matured plant and studied the interconnectedness of its roots, you have seen an example of a highly intricate network— one whose connections are so intertwined to the point that they have become indistinguishable from one another. Similarly, a well-developed brand complemented by genuine, interwoven relationships may work together catalytically to promote growth in an individual's career field.

With that in mind, you should never mistake surface-level networking for deep-rooted connections. Networking may be construed as someone attending an event and essentially flailing his arms out in an attempt to rub elbows with everyone present. Not a good look. In a similar vein, networking usually occurs in a mode of convenience, given that it commonly takes place in predetermined settings, with an expected end.

Connecting, on the other hand, necessitates effort beyond the predetermined setting and encompasses actually learning about someone and viewing that person not as a means to an end, but rather caring about who the person is as an individual, first and foremost. In like manner, you don't become important to someone until what's important to them becomes important to you. This factor is a byproduct of the basic principle of people not caring how much you know until they know how much you care.

Until you have made a connection, people do not officially become a part of your network. Hence, the rationale underlying the fact that the blue button on LinkedIn displays "Connect," instead of "Network." While a seemingly trivial detail, the site organizers were obviously aware of the chronology of building relationships in designing the interface. As such, the expansion of your network is largely contingent upon your ability to establish connections. Further pursuant to LinkedIn's nomenclature, when sending invitations to connect, you should consider editing the auto-generated message—especially if you don't know the person you seek to add. The obvious question is how many times do you think a given professional has seen the following message?

> *Hi John/Jane,*
>
> *I'd like to join your LinkedIn network.*
>
> *—Your Name*

Because such messaging is standard operating procedure, it will not help you to separate yourself from the masses or to establish a connection beyond cyberspace. If you have met the person before, it would not hurt to include a personal message to remind that individual of how you all were introduced. This advice may seem like a rudimentary practice, but you would be surprised at how little this tactic is used. This situation is your opportunity to kill two birds with one stone. Rather than sending the auto-generated invitation and *then* following up with an introductory note, you can maximize the opportunity by first wisely introducing yourself and then progressing from there.

Following this strategy, you will only need to rehash on the pleasantries before getting right down to business in a direct message. Who knows, the individual may even reach out to you beforehand in appreciation of the extra step that you took in adding a personal touch from the outset. If you take the initiative to follow-up, using these unconventional methods in cultivating genuine relationships, you will not have to scour job boards in search of opportunities to advance your career. They will figuratively come falling at your feet, if you are willing to put in the legwork on the front end.

The Lost Art

After an in-person meeting has been held, an opportunity is presented for bonds to be formed that can stand the test of time and distance. This process is initiated by your following-up with a handwritten thank-you note with mention of a topic you all discussed. If you do not learn anything else from this book, be sure and understand the power of a handwritten thank-you note, as opposed to digital correspondence. As legendary football coach Bill Curry once told me, "Will, there is nothing, I mean nothing, like a handwritten note."

Everyone you connect with should be treated with the utmost respect, which involves, among other things, not being slighted on the thank-you card front. The intern you met deserves a handwritten follow-up just as much as the executive with whom you spoke. Why? If you are an entry-level employee, or not far removed from this level, that intern will likely be closer to your peer group than the more seasoned professional. The elder professional may have more immediate hiring power, but that intern may very well reach a top leadership post in his own right, quite possibly before you do. In reality, he may end up hiring you one day!

Throughout his journey to reach a position of high authority, that individual will have likely explored numerous employment opportunities across multiple organizations. With each new stop came new phone numbers, new email addresses—you name it. He very well could have transferred all of his email contacts to each new account, but I strongly doubt it. It is more likely that he would have sooner held on to a tangible thank-you card instead.

If that seems a bit far-fetched, you should take a moment to consider how many emails you receive on a daily basis. A conservative estimate might be, oh say, 15? Some people may reach that number in an hour, but work with me in this instance. A mere follow-up email could get lost in the shuffle of important work-related correspondence and quickly forgotten about, even if the recipient responds. On the other hand, a well-written follow-up note will better resonate, if, for no other reason than, the recipient has to actually take the time to break the seal of the envelope and remove the card.

Such an action requires more time and fine motor skills than a mere left-click of the mouse. It also creates a memory that is hardly rivaled on a day-to-day basis. As a matter of fact, how often does *anything* handwritten come across your desk nowadays anyway? I'm willing to bet that you would not be able to match three of your closet coworkers with their respective handwriting styles in a blind test. With that in mind, a handwritten message, lined with gratitude, is sure to activate a sector of the recipient's brain that would otherwise remain dormant.

Eivaisla/iStock/Thinkstock

A handwritten message, lined with gratitude, is sure to activate a sector of the recipient's brain that would otherwise remain dormant.

Similarly, being on the receiving end of a handwritten thank-you note is no small achievement. It leads you to believe you made enough of an impression for someone to interrupt their daily work routine and craft a personal message appreciating you for your time. It is an act that sticks with you as you climb the ladder, especially when it comes from someone of high influence. You never lose touch with the feeling that it evokes. Hopefully, one day, you will decide to do the same thing for some other young professional who will be in your current shoes.

Tai even went as far as crafting a paper mural displaying every thank-you card he has received over the past 13 years! You never know what idiosyncrasies or values persist from one professional to another. As such, you should proceed with the expectation that someone is awaiting receipt of your thank-you card to add to his own wall.

I recall the day that I unexpectedly received a handwritten note from renowned football coach Mack Brown back in 2012. To this day, it remains as one of my most prized possessions. I remember how I felt when I opened that burnt-orange card, emblazoned with a Texas Longhorn, and read the personalized message within. This act meant a great deal to me, not because of Brown's stature, but because of the genuineness of the gesture itself. Consistent with the essence of connecting, it was composed by a selfless individual who epitomizes the value of establishing genuine relationships. His actions prompted me to write this portion of *The Blueprint*, which essentially crowns him as the featured architect for this section.

Up to this point in the book, the importance of planting seeds and nurturing them to form quality alliances have been covered. Once your relationships begin to blossom, the focus will shift to sustaining their vitality and productiveness. As the ties deepen, methods by which you may continually enrich your interactions and benefit each other should begin to present themselves. This is prompted by the frequency of which you share correspondence with or see those individuals you hold in high esteem, better known as touch points. Increasing your touch points enables you to glean keen insight on how you may positively impact other individuals on levels that transcend the norm.

Substantial touch points afford inside track access to what interests people over and above tasks that are directly associated with their job duties. What are their hobbies? What is their favorite book genre? Among others, the ability to answer these types of questions, combined with the initiative to act upon them generously, serves to strengthen the union exponentially. In that regard, you should consider purchasing a gift card or sending a book in accordance with the interests you perceived, expecting nothing in return. In this way, you become a branch of a fruit-bearing tree. And so the harvest begins…

FOUNDATIONAL FOOTINGS

Branding & Blossoming

VI. Plant positive seeds in the hearts and minds of those with whom you connect.

FOUNDATIONAL FOOTINGS

Part II: Cultivating Your Career Field

Hunter-Gatherers
IV. Seek out resources that help build your career capital.

Protecting the Head Coach
V. Allow your leader to excel by being excellent.

Branding & Blossoming
VI. Plant positive seeds in the hearts and minds of those with whom you connect.

PART III
Reaping the Harvest

You have made it to the home stretch. Your mentality is in tip-top shape. You have learned how to operate in your role at a high level, craft a distinguishable personal brand, and foster meaningful relationships. The next stage is to transition to the portion of the process most individuals elect to skip to before molding their mentality and focusing their full attention on existing responsibilities. Because you have followed the steps in the intended order, it is now time to feast on the fruits of your labor.

CHAPTER 7
Jersey Swap

*In this rare case, you are playing
for the name on the back of the
jersey. It just so happens
to be someone else's.*

If I asked you to name all the influential figures you *know* in your industry, I am sure you would be able to rattle off countless people you know...of. Would the people you named actually know you, or do you just know of them? In other words, would they vouch for you as a reference, or would you have to remind them of the time, date, place, latitude, longitude, degrees, and minutes, before they recalled even making your acquaintance? See the difference? As aspiring professionals, we often place great emphasis on making as many contacts as possible. That is all well and good, but how many of these people would actually go to bat for you?

All factors considered, young professionals are expected to cultivate relationships with prominent individuals who will endorse their competencies. A practical depiction of this factor would be someone of clout allowing you to parade around in a jersey with his name on the back of it, clearly representing him everywhere you go. Do you have anyone in your network who would let you wear his jersey? Try one of them on for size, and see if it fits. Conceivably, because a loose-fitting jersey could detract from your production in the course of a game, you need to make sure that it is tailor-made for you and not a hand-me-down.

The aforementioned analogy reinforces the following point: Everyone you meet will not be interested in your personal or professional development. That is just a cold hard fact, no matter how much you wish otherwise. Thus, it is imperative to nurture existing relationships with those individuals, irrespective of their professional stature, who do have your best interests at heart. Chances are they will be able to connect you with twice as many people than you could ever reach through cold-calling or uncultivated relationships.

You could easily fall victim to "over-networking" by stretching yourself too thin, while attempting to meet everyone under the sun, rather than reaping the harvest of the relationships that have already been planted in fertile ground. These existing seeds will eventually sprout and branch out, essentially growing your network without any undue effort on your part.

Each time one of your contacts makes a move, so do you. This situation is how six degrees of separation begins to dwindle down to about one or two. Similarly, that's why it is of paramount importance to build rapport with actual people and not mere titles or affiliations. As with player trades and student-athlete transfers in sport, the name on the front of the jersey may change, but individuals carry the name on the back of it wherever they go.

Arguably, the last thing you want to do is be caught sporting an outdated jersey (not to be confused with a throwback). Accordingly, your relationships must be able to withstand your contacts' potential job changes and moves throughout the industry. If you are enthralled

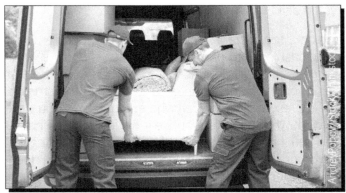

Each time one of your contacts makes a move, so do you.

solely by someone's position at a particular stop, you stand the chance of getting left behind with an inactive email address when that person leaves that position. Should this occur, any job recommendation you wish to have sent forth on your behalf will likely be returned to you as "undeliverable."

The Blueprint – Leadership Perspective

Forward Management (© Tai M. Brown)

❑ **PHASE #3: AFFIRMATION**

9. Do You Fit My Jersey – *Can your staff walk in public with a jersey that has your name on the back of it?* Accountability. Your staff represents you. Do you feel comfortable sending them out into the world with your reputation in their hands? If you have done your job in creating and maintaining an accountable, desirable, productive, and enterprising environment, then your staff should represent you well.

The Great Exchange

Thinking back on the following vignette, it is pretty remarkable how everything transpired and what came of the relationship that evolved from this fateful encounter. The scenario occurred during my first semester as a graduate student at Baylor. I was attending my first home football game. Of course, I was in Tai's hip pocket the whole time, because I did not really know anyone. We had arrived early to get set up to sell game programs. It was an evening game, if my memory serves me correctly, and Tai was showing me around historic Floyd Casey Stadium.

Prior to the start of the season, I informed Tai that my mentor, Dr. Jamil Northcutt, had an acquaintance who worked in Baylor Athletics with whom he wanted to connect me. He was referring to none other than renowned athletic performance coach Kaz Kazadi. I had yet to meet him in the few weeks I'd been on campus. Because he runs his program somewhat like a mafia cell, it was not as though I could have just shown up at his office door with baked goods.

Subsequently, Tai comes up with the bold idea to get me on the field before the teams warmed up. Coach Kaz would surely be there mentally and physically preparing himself for the upcoming contest. I was kind of anxious as we were walking toward the gridiron. Prior to setting foot on the turf, I had never been on a collegiate football field so close to kickoff time. The excitement around the impending game was palpable.

In the distance, I could see the silhouette of a muscle-bound figure moving very rapidly and efficiently. We proceeded in the direction of it. Tai and I came within 10 feet, ineffectively acting as if we had some business down there. Yet, Coach Kaz never acknowledged our existence. Tai greets him. Nothing.

Tai then attempts to work in an introduction for me. Still no acknowledgment. Only slow and controlled breaths emanating from Coach Kaz as he began another stretch. Tai brazenly continues on and deftly mentions, "This is Jamil Northcutt's guy."

Just like the dog in Ivan Pavlov's classical conditioning experiment, Coach Kaz immediately rouses at the sound of a familiar stimulus to the tune of a pachyderm professional's name. He quickly analyzes Tai for verification, looks at me, nods his head slightly, and resumes his warm-up. And that was that.

As I alluded to previously, I ended up working for Coach Kaz for two years. The resounding impact of his influence has been nothing short of extraordinary. Absent this initial encounter, and in part thanks to Tai, I am dubious as to whether I would have even been deemed as worthy of mere eye contact in the entire two years that I spent on campus.

Many fans would arrive to the stadium that evening, donning an array of jerseys in support of the players representing their beloved institutions. Not to be outdone, I happened to be sporting a most unique jersey of my own. The instant Coach Kaz realized there was an abstract, Northcutt-laden jersey covering my Baylor polo, everything changed.

It stood out enough to garner the attention of someone who would have otherwise regarded me as vapor in that moment. That's how I felt for a minute at least. On the other hand, because the jersey I was sporting was held in such high esteem, I was able to regain my dignity through even the slightest of gestures—a head nod. That was all of the validation I was going to get, which certainly sufficed for me. In short, the sheer power of a jersey swap with a pachyderm professional had already flexed its muscle before I was made aware of its exhaustive capacity. (An explanation concerning what exactly a pachyderm professional is will be detailed in the next chapter, by the way.)

I take great pride in all of the names that I have written on my back, figuratively speaking. Aside from my family, I represent a number of high-profile professionals who took the time to personally invest in my career. What was once a jersey with a single name on the back of it now resembles Joseph's multicolor coat in a sense, with each name retaining its significant value, despite new stitching. These eponymous professionals enable me to do some serious name-dropping, as I seek to find common ground and cultivate meaningful relationships with new people.

I estimate 90 percent of my entire network originated from about three to four core contacts. As for the other 10 percent? I could have saved myself a lot of time and trouble had I asked my core contacts if they already knew the individuals in that 10 percentile. This revelation showed that I was hustling backwards. As such, I began to help my network help me. With some name-drops in tow, I would circle back with my self-begotten contacts, and the conversation would immediately take off. An actual relationship would then begin to materialize, because they could now associate me with someone of influence. I learned my lesson fairly quickly after this situation reoccurred a few times.

I began sharing every event I was planning to attend with my core network and was sure to highlight any notable individuals who were expected to be in attendance. To this day, since implementing this strategy, I have yet to visit any institution or conference without being armed with at least one or two standing relationships. Nowadays, I will not attend so much as a high school basketball game without first asking a core contact, "Whom do we know here?"

With that consideration in mind, aside from the networking perks, there is a great deal of accountability and responsibility that comes along with parading around in someone's jersey. You must present yourself in a manner that is complementary of the person who put you in position to make a play. Their brand is now your brand and vice versa. The last thing you want to do is embarrass someone who put their reputation on the line for you. You will obviously place yourself in a difficult position, but, in turn, will also impede the ability of your mentor to refer other quality individuals. How will this affect the other up-and-coming professionals who will require a valid reference?

Per your insensitivity to guarding the throne, you will have relegated a well-respected professional to "the boy who cried wolf." The strength of his voucher will no longer be taken into serious consideration, as he endeavors to facilitate opportunities for others in the future. The umbrella that was sheltering you has now been flipped inside out. Arguably, everyone knows how big of a hassle it is trying to get those things straightened out.

Furthermore, your road to recovery from a major faux pas will be far rockier than that of the jersey lender you represent. He will likely be well off into his career, just as you are embarking on your own. Accordingly, you have a tight window of opportunity and an even slimmer margin for error. But hey, no pressure, no diamonds.

FOUNDATIONAL FOOTINGS

Jersey Swap

VII. Represent those who vouch for you as if you wear a jersey bearing their name instead of yours.

CHAPTER 8
Pachyderm Professionals

Raise your hand if you are tired of hearing, "It's not what you know, it's who you know."

"And everybody's hands go UP!"
—T-Pain

There. It's unanimous. Let's take it a step further. It is not so much whom you know; it's more a matter of who knows you *and* with whom do they associate you.

Upon entering any field of endeavor, you first must identify who the influencers are at the micro- and macro-levels. In other words, which individuals comprise a "Committee of One," as Coach Teaff likes to refer to it. On the other hand, if you are more of a catchphrase fan, who can make one call and that's all? These individuals are your pachyderm professionals, or for the purposes of this chapter—elephants.

The behemoths mentioned here are not typically found at the petting zoo or seen on the Discovery Channel. Nevertheless, there is a great deal to be learned from pachyderm *professionals* both in their natural habitats and abroad. As they walk among us, their mere presence makes them difficult to overlook.

For example, when you think of an elephant, similar to the euphemism of an elephant being in the room, what comes to mind? Logically speaking, you see an imposing figure that carries a great deal of weight. That assessment holds true in the following sense—the weight aspect pertaining more so to power.

Elephants can get the ball rolling up a steep incline with ease or, conversely, halt it on a 45 degree slope with very little effort. If resistance does persist, it is usually in the form of a ploy, in order to not blatantly undermine someone's authority. As badly as it may sound, that is how the real world works, at times. Because job titles do not always signify elephants, you need to be diligent in your search to correctly identify them.

The Blueprint – Leadership Perspective

Forward Management (© Tai M. Brown)

❏ **PHASE #3: AFFIRMATION**

10. Walk With the Elephants – *Would you bring your staff around influential leaders in the industry?* In order to be successful, you must walk with the elephants. This can be rephrased as, in order to be successful, you must be around successful people. Elephants are big, imposing animals that everyone notices. In every industry, there are influential leaders who are considered the elephants of the profession. Learning from these leaders happens best when you are amongst them. As you have trained your staff to wear your jersey comfortably, allow them to accompany you as you walk with the elephants of your industry.

Being connected to leaders of this caliber can greatly impact your career, both personally and professionally. Nevertheless, you must consider what enabled these people to tip the proverbial scales in their favor. They likely walked in the shadows of elephants of their time and capitalized on the opportunities that ensued. Association breeds similarity, so if you align yourself with successful people, you enhance your chances to be the next successful person.

Elephants know who they are. It's tough to carry that much weight around without knowing you are shaking life a little bit. Thus, it is an exclusive privilege to walk alongside them. They have strong networks of human capital that have been cultivated and nurtured over time. Quite honestly, their de facto networks are much larger than they often realize in light of the vast collection of people who know *of* them, but have yet to connect. You stand to benefit most from this phenomenon, if you associate with the right people.

This particular strategy was covered aptly in the last chapter, Jersey Swap. For the purposes of this chapter, however, it is only the tip of the iceberg. While sporting the jersey of an influencer has many advantages, there is another level of influence that involves you being in the physical presence of a pachyderm professional amongst his peers. While ideal, it is obviously not always the most practical way in which you are able to go about expanding your network. It all depends on location, location, location. Furthermore, as you learned from my experiences with Coach Kaz in the previous chapter, some elephants carry so much weight that you don't even need them around to make meaningful associations.

Nevertheless, when you actually have a chance to physically walk alongside them, you will begin to pick up on the modest characteristics that typically comprise their miens. These features refer to the seemingly trivial gestures and political skill that serve to aggrandize their effectiveness and outward perception among people-watchers like you and me. Eventually, you will also come to find out what the stitched text size is of the name actually written above your shoulder blades.

For example, although I was a graduate assistant at the time, Coach Teaff was always great about introducing me to his high-profile coaching and administrative peers. From current coaches, such as Mark Richt to the legendary NFL Hall-of-Famer Mike Singletary, he always made sure to involve me in conversations. It would then be up to me to make an impression and develop the possible relationship from there. He had done his part. Frankly, he certainly did not have to do as much as he did. I later found that, aside from the existing relationships he had in place, it was the manner in which he introduced me that made all the difference. I will elaborate in the example to follow.

Taking an unworthy companion around your mother can be a major faux pas. Similarly, you cannot expect respected professionals to share their network with you if you aren't polished and proven. You must proceed as if every day is a continuous job interview, because chances are it is. The value of walking with elephants and the opportunities they can lead to cannot be overstated. It is important to note, however, that you must get your weight up before getting in stomp with a pachyderm professional.

Elevating With Elephants

An old saying claims that birds of a feather flock together. Accordingly, it should come as no surprise that elephants of a herd share words. (Note: If that corny phrase ever becomes famous, remember where you read it first!) In layman's terms, peers and counterparts have a higher proclivity to gravitate toward one another. That is not to say they do not interact with other individuals who have titles and roles that are different from their own. Nonetheless, conversations require far less effort to carry on when there are shared interests and backgrounds.

If you have ever attended a conference at which professionals of varying ranks are present, you have likely seen this scenario live in living color. In working for the American Football Coaches Association, whose flagship event is the annual convention, I have witnessed this occurrence on a yearly basis since 2013, with no indication of it changing course. We as young professionals, fully aware of our professional standing, should be careful not to interrupt exchanges between high-ranking individuals. Nevertheless, there is an art to strategically positioning ourselves to pounce on a few seconds of potential facetime, should an opportunity present itself.

We may as well be kids on the playground, vying to get selected for schoolyard kickball. That is, of course, unless you happen to be best friends with one of the team captains. If that's the case, you are home free! This is the sort of confidence that tends to consume me when I am walking alongside pachyderm professional and co-contributor, Tai M. Brown. Though he has introduced me to more high-ranking individuals than I can count, one of our more resounding escapades took place during my first visit to the NACDA (National Association of Collegiate Directors of Athletics) Convention in Orlando, Florida, in 2015.

We were walking down a corridor at NACDA, when Tai spotted Jamie Pollard, his friend and the Director of Athletics at Iowa State University. I had yet to meet Mr. Pollard, so naturally I was very happy about the imminent opportunity at hand. What ensued from this encounter and its carryover impact turned out to be a most pleasant surprise.

The two exchanged pleasantries, and Tai proceeded to give me somewhat of an informal introduction. After relaying my name and affiliation, Tai went on to say that I reminded him of Mr. Pollard, who was standing amongst us of course. I was pleasantly blindsided to say the least. The most I would have thought I had in common with a sitting athletic director was maybe a shoe size.

Tai went on to recall a PowerPoint presentation he assisted Mr. Pollard with at an annual meeting the year prior. In giving the presentation, Tai observed Mr. Pollard *noticing* the slightest of mistakes on one of the slides. A single bullet point was slightly misaligned. Furthermore, as Tai continued on, while Mr. Pollard maintained his composure for the remainder of the presentation, he could tell Pollard was none too pleased by the error. With me being equally fastidious in Tai's eyes, he craftily made the connection between Mr. Pollard and me.

While duly pleasing in the moment, I figured this would be all that would come of it. I was sure that Mr. Pollard had far more important things on his mind than sharing a trait with an individual who was three months removed from being an intern. I was wrong. Dead wrong.

The next day, as Tai and I were headed to a session, we spotted Mr. Pollard across the hall having a seated talk with a fellow athletic director. Not wanting to impose, we quickly averted our attention and pressed forward. Just as we were about to exit his peripheral vision, Pollard paused his conversation and playfully called out to me, "Hey Will, let's make sure we have those details straight!"

I was utterly awestruck in that moment. Not only did he briefly halt a conversation with a respected peer, he remembered my name and made sure his statement was audible in the midst of a noisy hallway. First and foremost, this act alone placed him in the upper echelon of pachyderm professionals in my book, given that, in my mind, this type of treatment was not an anomaly or specific to me. It's just the type of person Mr. Pollard is beyond his title.

Furthermore, I doubt that I would have even met Mr. Pollard had I not been walking alongside an elephant at NACDA. I mean, how clever of Tai to provide an introduction substantial enough to be recalled by Mr. Pollard a full day later? There were over 5,000 sport professionals in attendance. In all likelihood, he had encountered a number of other people since we'd last spoken 24 hours earlier.

In this scenario, I was awarded an on-the-spot jersey endowment by a pachyderm professional in the presence of a fellow elephant. The wisdom I took from this experience is two-fold. For starters, there is most definitely an art to making a lasting introduction (that may be a slight oxymoron, but you get what I'm saying). The informal introduction is essentially what humanized Pollard for me and caused any perceived barriers between us to come crashing down. Everyone was instantly made to feel comfortable, which opened the door for Tai to slip me right on in, as Pollard reminisced and laughed.

Furthermore, in the midst of all this going on, I had to be perceptive of what was transpiring or risk missing the call for a golden opportunity. Oftentimes, names are forgotten, and associations lost in the abyss the minute you turn to walk away, especially among high-ranking officials whom everyone is vying to meet. As was discussed in the previous chapter, Jersey Swap, this factor is what causes you to have to remind them of the time, date, place, latitude, longitude, and so on, before they recall making your acquaintance. It does not have to be this way, however.

At some point in the future, you will require assistance from someone of great influence and social skill to pull off meaningful connections on the first attempt. In which case, you will be able to ascertain both how form-fitting your endowed jersey is, as well as how adept your pachyderm professional is at helping you show it off. Flaunt it with flare.

As you venture to mold your brand in the form of those individuals whom you admire, you cannot afford to let any stratagem, mannerism, or good quality bypass your senses. As such, you need to be prepared to learn from every experience and adopt the qualities that will make the external perception of you mirror the one churning on the inside. This gap can only be filled by learning what successful people do to sustain success. Similar to the music industry, you are likely to identify some one-hit wonders in your profession. According to Coach Kaz, people can be good by accident. On the other hand, greatness cannot be stumbled upon. The latter attribute comes from training your mind, both in theory and in practice. In theory, you can accrue a wealth of knowledge on best practices through observation alone. Nonetheless, the most rewarding aspect of this dynamic arises from putting the tactics you have observed into practice and witnessing their effects for yourself.

As is noted in the next chapter, Forward Together, one of the overarching themes of *The Blueprint* is recognizing that everyone is important. If you inhale oxygen and exhale carbon dioxide, like all human beings, surely you know what it feels like to be "big-timed" by someone you admire or hold in high esteem. I once found my business card left lying on a table where the former occupants once sat. Talk about a deflating experience. Such episodes are what make having prominent individuals treat you as the most important person in the world so special.

Elephants know who they are.

Coach Teaff embodies this remarkable trait to no end. From watching him discreetly check badges during conversations to address everyone by name, to his dexterity in directing meetings filled with high-profile FBS head coaches, I have gleaned a wealth of knowledge simply by watching him "move and shake." I cannot count the number of "aha!" moments I have experienced in identifying the many "it" factors specific to him. I even began infusing these skills into encounters of my own, in hopes of them yielding similar results. The effort works like a charm every time.

Though many individuals regard making new contacts as an expected end when walking with the elephants, if you view this outcome as the sole benefit, you have only seen the tip of the iceberg. In other words, you have failed to acknowledge the gargantuan mass of greatness below the surface. Such intangibles are what will provide the most benefit in the long term. Accordingly, be careful not to allow them to float past you.

FOUNDATIONAL FOOTINGS

Pachyderm Professionals

VIII. In order to be successful, you must be around successful people.

CHAPTER 9
Forward Together

*As iron sharpens iron, so one
person sharpens another.*

—Proverbs 27:17 (NIV)

There are two "Cs" essential to reaching success and sustaining it in perpetuity—competitiveness and compassion. Obviously, you have to be competitive. On the other hand, you also have to be compassionate. As you navigate the labyrinth that is the process, you should avoid neglecting other individuals who may be at a stage of development that is different from yours. If you perceive someone is, in fact, deficient in an area in which you are well-versed, it is incumbent of you to step in and help them along. It is never too early to begin replenishing the storehouse with the wealth of knowledge you have gained.

When an experienced professional bestows wisdom upon you, a sense of reverence naturally surfaces. That same lesson resonates more, however, when someone in your cohort reaffirms it with relatable experiences. Sound familiar? It's like that parent versus peer phenomenon.

You should help your peers avoid the pitfalls you may have succumbed to in the course of your own development. They will likely reinforce the soundness of your guidance and reciprocate the favor, when applicable. After all, the former is what led to the creation of this book. After gleaning much of the same information from an array of elite professionals, I began plugging these principles into my career development.

With each bit of positive feedback came an increased vigor to learn more. For me, the most gratifying experience was taking an introspective look at my own personal growth and development. Although I had a good foundation, I still found myself far behind the curve when I began my career. I thought to myself: "There is no way I'm the only one who didn't know all this stuff." I am too competitive to have accepted such a disconcerting truth. As a result, I started writing this book. My goal in crafting *The Blueprint* was to do as Tai often says and "put it back in the bucket." The training I received early on in my career was exceptional, and I count it as nothing short of a blessing. Why not share it?

In the same vein, until you are able to develop talent and refer quality individuals for job opportunities, you have yet to reach your full potential. As you refine your brand, your influence within the industry will begin to increase. As such, at that point, you need to put it to good use. With influence comes power, and power begets responsibility. The onus is now upon you to extend the cover of the umbrella that ushered you into the domain of the influential. Otherwise, everything your influencers did for you will have been for naught. It is your responsibility to share the network, the knowledge, whatever you have to offer. Ralph Waldo Emerson once said, "Be an opener of doors for such as come after you." In other words, set the doorstopper on your way in.

It may seem counterintuitive, but staff recruitment often initiates at the entry-level—the provenance of young professionals' careers. They link with like-minded individuals in their cohort who are trying to find their place in the industry, just as they are. You should seek to identify complementary talent among your peers early in your career progression. Who knows? You may end up hiring or working for one of these people one day. Likewise, it will save time in both the interviewing and subsequent onboarding process as a working knowledge of the expectations will already be in place. He will walk in the door with the white gloves on!

This strategy of early coalition-building fosters an environment of idea-sharing, new opportunities, and downright genuine relationships to build upon. To that point, before even securing my first full-time job,

I had assisted three classmates in securing employment with reputable organizations; namely, the American Football Coaches Association, Conference USA, and (Leigh) Steinberg Sports & Entertainment.

I take great pride in my standing to provide sound references for other individuals in the early stages of my career. None of this would have been possible, however, had I not learned from the giants whose shoulders I first stood upon. My goal is to put it back in the bucket until it runneth over.

The Blueprint – Leadership Perspective

Forward Management (© Tai M. Brown)

❏ **PHASE #3: AFFIRMATION**

11. Putting It Back in the Bucket – *Is your staff ready to mentor others as you have mentored them?* Dipping in the proverbial bucket of experience and mentorship helped you get to where you are today. You have given back to that bucket by helping others to be successful through creating and maintaining an environment for leadership development. To ensure a similar outcome, teach this concept to your staff so that when they become leaders, they too will create and maintain their own environment for successful leadership.

Growth. Development. Influence. These are the sheer beauty of the process.

Most accomplishments pale in comparison to the realization that you have made significant strides in a given area and are now feasting on the fruits of your labor. Conversely, professionals often lament about what they wish they had known in the past compared to what they now know. Don't get me wrong; there is no substitute for on-the-job experience. Nevertheless, this hackneyed complaint is often grounded in a person's mentality more so than the knowledge germane to that individual's profession.

Learning is ubiquitous. It happens daily in some shape or form. It is not every day, however, that you experience a mental paradigm shift in how you go about your business. That is a level most people do not reach until they are well into their careers. By then, they have already bumped their heads on the glass ceiling multiple times. Windex, anyone? At this point a light comes on, and they then realize they have gone through the motions during the most critical points in their career, most notably, beginning as a young professional.

But, not you. If you mind the counsel of *The Blueprint* early on, you are sure to get ahead of the curve. In turn, you will be able to bring others up to speed with tactful mentorship. To that point, every concept in this book was imparted by someone else in theory and/or practice. The only modicum of credit I can lay claim to is interpreting these vital concepts for those individuals who are just beginning their ascension. By following the precepts outlined in *The Blueprint*, you will find that you are beginning on a solid foundation as you build to reach new heights. Thus, as your altitude increases, make an effort to raise as you rise by reaching back and pulling the next person up. While you should never seek reciprocation for such acts, according to Sir Isaac Newton's third law, "For every action, there is an equal and opposite reaction." Thus, you may rightfully expect a return on the selfless investments you make into other people.

In other words, your career will be affected by the forces acting upon you and those aspects you exact, in turn. Over time, the term "mentor" has evolved to become synonymous with trusted advisor, friend, and counselor. Mentoring is the cornerstone of human development and involves the selfless investment of time, energy, and resources to positively impact the lives of others. It is the lifeblood of our livelihoods. In reality, without its continued circulation, we are destined to flatline. Looking back, I believe that I was nearing this point until Tai stepped in and resuscitated my lifeline of writing—one that had been lying dormant since my English teacher retired after my junior year of high school.

Tai's uncanny ability to evoke every individual's truest form of human expression and channel it into productive avenues is what catapults him into the upper echelon of modern-day mentors. Prior to going through his school of thought, I often wondered what he got out of these acts. It was not as though the young professionals he was advising were paying for his services (as if they could afford it).

The more I thought about it, the more I came to realize that you may run out of money, but the well of influence will never run dry, if you dig deep enough. Your career trajectory will be impacted most by the individuals you are influenced by and the succeeding influence you disseminate among others.

Raise as you rise by reaching back and pulling the next person up.

The law of conservation of energy states that energy—or in this instance, influence—can neither be created nor destroyed. Rather, it transforms from one form to another. Energy exists in two basic forms: potential and kinetic. Potential energy refers to any type of stored energy, while kinetic energy is manifested in the form of movement. The mode in which these two energy forms relate to one another is analogous to an engine and its powering of an automobile.

A parked car in working condition possesses a great deal of stored or potential energy. All factors considered, with the proper stimulus, it could go from "zero to 100 real quick." Until the engine is triggered by the ignition switch, however, the energy remains stored. In other words, it has all the *potential* in the world, but has yet to go anywhere. In like manner, until a mentor ignites the powerful engine hidden within you, you remain as that parked car—a mass of stored, unlimited potential capable of gyrating movement.

It is no secret that effectual leadership can be transformative, revolutionary even. It can be powerful enough to spark sweeping changes and paradigms shifts in the consciences of those impacted. Such seismic shifts take place in organizations spanning from Girl Scouts, to corporations, to entire nations. In fact, the world is right in the middle of the technology revolution now, and the change it brings on a month-to-month basis is even quite remarkable.

The term "revolution" speaks to the act of revolving, similar to the circular movement the wheels of a vehicle make after they have transformed their potential energy into kinetic movement. Furthermore, you should consider the RPM gauge that may be found on either side of your car's speedometer (as illustrated by the following image). The RPM acronym simply stands for "revolutions per minute." A quick glance at the RPM display will reveal static, single-digit numbers, positioned behind a needle correlating to your speed.

What most people fail to acknowledge, however, is the print left of the RPM acronym—the print that reads "x 1000." The multiplier. "Two" revolutions suddenly become two-*thousand* revolutions, marking a significant difference, when the multiplier is taken into account. As such, the once, seemingly meaningless numbers have taken on all-new value.

The single-digits represent what your career could amount to without the necessary attention applied by a mentor, i.e., an amplifier. Negligible. Nevertheless, as you just discovered, these stand-alone digits are not indicative of their true value. A closer look reveals the augmenter, or aug*mentor*, whose transformative value likely went unnoticed initially. The gauge's multiplier is metaphorically analogous to how effectual mentorship jumpstarts your career and the significant influence to be realized by its discover-ability.

Consistent with the example, mentors are the catalysts who get you up to speed to "move the needle." They are the vehicles by which forward progress is made. As such, they serve as energy transfer points for the proliferation of leaders who will begin cranking out mentees of their own. Still, this phenomenon revolves around the consideration of "Why?", which is the key to unlocking your full potential, in orbital fashion that is best described as the circle of leadership. This cycle, and this cycle alone, is what accelerates a revolution, both in the primary and secondary sense.

Nevertheless, you should remain mindful of the fact you are in the driver's seat in pursuit of your destiny. It is analogous to driving bumper cars, if you really think about it. While in the driver's seat, distractions may emerge, attempting to knock you off course. Fortunately, you will never fully leave the track. You may be diverted slightly, or even brought to a transient halt, but there are guardrails in place to keep you from vacating the track altogether.

These guardrails are your standards, and the more you grow as a professional, the thicker they become—so much so that they begin to jut inward and encapsulate you to the point where there is no room for negative influences to deter you from staying on the straight and narrow. At this point, it's just you and the open road. Zoom, zoom.

Trust in your ability to exceed even your own expectations and grasp everything God has laid out for you. Hopefully the principles that have been outlined in *The Blueprint* will assist you in establishing a standard for both your personal and professional life. Absent standards, everything becomes arbitrary and amenable to change. Thus, a standard-driven mentality must permeate every facet of your life, from your faith to your health.

You should decide what you want your legacy to be and how you will go about establishing it. Visualize your goals and choose to be confident in your ability to reach and even speed past them. Always remember that vision is a function of the heart, while sight is a function of the eyes. Accordingly, if you want to see beyond the surface, you must put your heart into it.

May your influence outlive you.

FOUNDATIONAL FOOTINGS

Forward Together

IX. Raise as you rise by reaching back and pulling the next person up.

FOUNDATIONAL FOOTINGS

Part III: Reaping the Harvest

Jersey Swap

VII. Represent those who vouch for you as if you wear a jersey bearing their name instead of yours.

Pachyderm Professionals

VIII. In order to be successful, you must be around successful people.

Forward Together

IX. Raise as you rise by reaching back and pulling the next person up.

FOUNDATIONAL FOOTINGS
The Blueprint for a Successful Career

As young professionals, we are heavily consumed with laying the groundwork for what we hope are lengthy, successful careers. *The Blueprint* was crafted as an illustration to help guide your career construction. Before establishing a foundation to build upon, your footings must be firmly entrenched. Use the following principles to solidify your professional platform—not only to uphold yourself—but other people as well.

Part I: The Lay of the Land

Buy Your Way In
I.   Make a deliberate decision to hold yourself accountable for your thoughts, actions, and the service you provide to those you work for.

Leggo My Ego
II. Until you know that you don't always know, you will not know what you are capable of knowing and, thus, accomplishing.

Be Where You Are
III. Aspire to make your contribution indispensable.

Part II: Cultivating Your Career Field

Hunter-Gatherers
IV. Seek out resources that help build your career capital.

Protecting the Head Coach
V. Allow your leader to excel by being excellent.

Branding & Blossoming
VI. Plant positive seeds in the hearts and minds of those with whom you connect.

Part III: Reaping the Harvest

Jersey Swap
VII. Represent those who vouch for you as if you wear a jersey bearing their name instead of yours.

Pachyderm Professionals
VIII. In order to be successful, you must be around successful people.

Forward Together
IX. Raise as you rise by reaching back and pulling the next person up.

BONUS CHAPTER
The Inspiration

Hopefully, by now, I have made it crystal clear that I am very passionate about the process. Through personal anecdotes in the preceding chapters, I have sought to paint a mosaic of an imperfect young professional, who literally fell in love with the journey. In this final section, I try to share, in uninterrupted detail, how the process, along with prayer, literally changed my life.

Pre-Process

Prior to graduating from the University of Mississippi in May 2012, I had already made up my mind that I wanted to try my hand in Texas and transition into sport administration. Those desires led me to apply to Baylor University. Two full months before commencement, I received a letter in the mail approving my admission into the Baylor Sport Management master's program.

Graduate school, in and of itself, is not cheap. Tuition at Baylor, whether undergraduate or post-graduate, is not exactly a drop in the bucket, either. Because I was aware of this fact before submitting my application, I took the initiative to apply for a graduate assistantship that would cover tuition, provide a monthly stipend, and afford me pertinent work experience in sport.

Unfortunately, according to the letter, I was not approved for a single assistantship. I was devastated. The initial high I had felt instantly began to fade. I considered delaying my enrollment, as well as all sorts of my other potential options. Though slightly discouraged, I was at least thankful to have an opportunity to continue my education, whenever it may come.

As odd as it may seem, with an undergraduate degree on the horizon and a post-graduate acceptance letter in hand, my future still seemed uncertain to me. All the while, my family had been planning a trip to Dallas, Texas, for a family reunion on my mother's side of the family. A little help from MapQuest alerted me to the fact that Waco, home of Baylor University, was a little over 100 miles down the road. Given my family's financial situation at the time, I had to make the absolute most of this trip.

Prior to the getaway, I contacted the director of the Baylor Sport Management Program, Dr. Jeffrey Petersen, to inform him of my travel plans and to request if I could visit with him on campus. He heartily agreed and even mentioned an organization that was considering reviving their graduate assistantship program—one that had been inactive since 2004. There was one potential opening. A screening interview had been set.

It was on a Friday afternoon, when my family reunion was coming to a close, that my father agreed to drive me down to Waco. Once we arrived, I connected with Dr. Petersen, and he showed me around campus, as we discussed the sport management program. Following our tour, I was directed to a room in the Student Life Center, and it was there I first met Tai M. Brown, Director of Education at the American Football Coaches Association. He put me through the most rigorous interview that I have ever experienced, even to this day. I powered through it nonetheless, and before I knew it, I was headed back to Dallas.

Three weeks passed without any feedback from my interview, so naturally I began to feel a little anxious. I was oblivious to the fact Dr. Petersen had been pressing Tai regarding my candidacy. In retrospect, I learned that Tai had tabled my application due to the fact that he hadn't heard from me since our interview in terms of a follow-up missive.

Dr. Petersen, awestruck at my ignorance I'm sure, called and briefed me on the major faux pas that I had unknowingly committed. After we hung up, I nearly broke my keyboard, trying to craft a much-delayed follow-up note to Tai. Graciously, he accepted it and responded.

By late July, I still had not received word regarding whether I had been approved for the assistantship. Weeks prior, I'd chosen to confirm my fall semester attendance on the grounds of faith alone. Not surprisingly, I was beginning to get a little nervous, as the due date for tuition was fast approaching.

I had three days to provide some form of payment or risk having my schedule cancelled. Time was running out. Then came the moment of truth.

I was running an errand for my dad one dreary morning, when the phone rang. It was a caller from Waco, Texas. I was pleasantly surprised to hear Tai's voice on the line, and not someone from Baylor's accounts receivable office. He informed me that I would be hired on as a graduate assistant with the American Football Coaches Association. All glory to God!

Allow me to backtrack to fill in some important gaps. As I indicated previously, I had my heart set on having a career in strength and conditioning until the last semester of my senior year at Ole Miss. I was serving my internship at the Starnes training facility, when I decided to approach a gentleman by the name of Jamil Northcutt, Ph.D. I basically asked him what he did for a living, and his response immediately piqued my interest. He took me under his wing and gave me an inside look into the field of sport management. This encounter is what ultimately led me to begin applying to sport management programs, namely Baylor's. This is the point at which it gets interesting.

Unbeknownst to me, until Tai relayed the story, he and Dr. Northcutt met at a conference for the first time in the summer of 2012. This span was the same time period in which I was awaiting word from AFCA regarding the assistantship opportunity. Following a session at the conference, Tai told me he noticed an Ole Miss lapel pin donning a gentleman's sport coat and proceeded to introduce himself. It was none other than—you guessed it—Dr. Northcutt. They exchanged pleasantries, and Tai asked Dr. Northcutt if he knew of me. Being my mentor for all of three months, Dr. Northcutt took it from there and gave me a glowing recommendation.

Beyond my futile follow-up, I found that this impromptu exchange is what ultimately led Tai to bring me on at the AFCA that fateful fall. A single encounter between two erstwhile strangers is what jumpstarted my career; the rest has been detailed in the preceding pages. Oh, and did I mention Tai and Dr. Northcutt did not see each other in person for four years beyond that day? This is how I know there was a third, invisible guest in the midst of them.

Some individuals refer to my situation as luck, others as good fortune. For your benefit, I have included the phonetic pronunciation: FAVOR/'fāvər/.

The Process at Work

Moving ahead to February 2015. By now, I have completed my Master's degree, my AFCA graduate assistantship, and an internship with the Chick-fil-A Peach Bowl. I was on the prowl for full-time employment, but had only experienced marginal success until Googling "sports jobs in Atlanta" one day. I saw an opening with IMG College within their licensing arm (Collegiate Licensing Company). I submitted an application, and the individuals for whom I worked at the Chick-fil-A Peach Bowl readily recommended me for the position.

I was selected for the first round of interviews, and in my opinion, mine went really well. The people were great, and the sense of community in the office was palpable. I went home that night and wrote thank-you notes that were addressed to the three individuals with whom I interviewed. With a job offer from another company on the table by that time, I opted against snail mail to expedite the process. The next day, I drove back up to the office and hand-delivered the thank-you cards. I came to find this act went over really well (hint hint).

Next, came the second round of interviews on the following Wednesday, and like the initial round, the energy and feel were remarkable. Following my interview, I requested feedback within 48 hours, because I had to provide the other company with an answer soon.

Upon learning my hand-delivered notes had set me apart from the field, I elected to follow the same protocol for round two. My plan was to drop them off the next morning, Thursday, as I had before. There was a small problem, however. On unrelated terms, I was originally scheduled to meet with Dr. Billy Hawkins at the University of Georgia the preceding Tuesday—the day before my second interview. Due to inclement weather, we were forced to reschedule for Thursday morning. Yes, the same Thursday in question. I had to make a decision. Drop the cards off first and risk being late for the meeting, or head on down to UGA and figure out the rest on the back end? I opted for the latter.

I did not make it back to Atlanta until 4:30 p.m., when rush hour was at its height (as if I would know any differently). Though 5:00 p.m. was fast approaching, the typical close of business hour, I elected to try my luck at delivering the cards anyway. I was scheduled to fly out to Dallas, Texas, the next morning at 7 a.m. and would be gone for a week. It was now or never, or so it seemed.

I got one mile away from the office building when I received a call from Katie Craig of IMG Human Resources. This would be our first time speaking since my last interview.

> Katie: Hi Will! Do you have a couple of minutes?

> Me: Hey Katie, sure what's up?

> Katie: Well, the team is really interested in you, and they wanted to know if you could possibly come back in to meet with a couple more people.

> Me: Katie, you know I'd be glad to, but I'm flying to Dallas tomorrow, and I'll be gone for a week.

> Katie: Oh that's right, I remember you telling me that. Well, do you think there is any way you could hold off giving the other organization an answer for another week and a half or so?

> Me: I'm not sure if that's feasible, since I've been holding them out for two weeks already. But hey listen; I'm actually on the way to the IMG office right now. I...

> Katie (jokingly): Are you coming to drop off more thank-you notes, Will?

Me (sheepishly): Umm, maybe...

Katie: Well let me see if I can round up some team members and let them know you're already on your way. See you soon!

I arrived at the office, and Katie met me when I exited the elevator. We chatted for a few moments, and it wasn't long before a senior vice president at CLC entered the conversation. We then moved to her office to discuss specifics on what the job would entail, as well as gauge my general interest in the position.

I conveyed to her that I was very interested in the position. At that point, she proceeded to phone the managing director of CLC. We conducted an impromptu telephone conference, during which they assured me that they would extend an offer within the next 24 hours. Not expecting anything more that evening, I left the office and started for home. I got about two miles down the road, 10 minutes Atlanta traffic time, and the phone rang. IMG-CLC offered me a generous starting salary with full benefits! I could not do anything but thank God.

Reflecting back on the day's events, had it not been for the storm on Tuesday, I would have delivered my thank-you notes that Thursday morning instead of that evening. It wouldn't have been my time. God already had a set time for his will to be fulfilled; I only needed to be obedient.

There is a gap of about two and a half years between the first part and the second part of the preceding stories. Each time I reflect on these happenings, specifically on the vastly different protocols I followed, I get a breath of fresh air. The lack of a mere follow-up note is what almost cost me access into the sport industry, while persevering to follow-up like none other is what ultimately landed me my first full-time job.

It does go to show that it is not where you start, but where you finish. This precept is what we who are pursuing greatness refer to as the process. We love the process for the same reason we love sport. The comebacks. The upsets. The uncertainty of outcome. The mere possibility of the underdog rising to the challenge and defying the odds keeps us hungry for more. Given the challenges that we face in pursuit of our goals, beginning the process is no different. On the other hand, because we know we have a chance, we are relentless in seeing to it that our dreams are manifested. In other words, we just do what we do.

The uncertainty is the driving force behind all we do to achieve success. Because we have no idea where we may end up, we bust our tails in hopes of positioning ourselves for the most favorable opportunities possible. Absent the uncertainty, the career grind can become dull. Thus, you should embrace the value of the unknown as you navigate the process.

After all, you have *The Blueprint* to help guide you.

AFTERWORD

In the fall of 2003, a young man walked into my office and introduced himself as our new intern at the American Football Coaches Association. As a former college football coach, I have employed a number of young men seeking to make headway in the sport profession in one way or another. However, the minute I shook Tai M. Brown's hand, I knew he was special. During my coaching career, I worked with young men from all walks of life. And after a while, I became proficient at seeing beyond the surface to discover the true essence of the young men I was leading. Although I had transitioned to my role as Executive Director when Tai came into my life, I retained my knack for peeling away the layers when encountering others.

Maybe, it was his customary, "Greetings!" accompanied by his unmistakable smile that grabbed my attention. Maybe, it was the look in his eye—one that communicated passion and a desire to make a significant impact. In 2016, as I step aside from my role as Executive Director, I am humbled to say that Tai has far exceeded my expectations.

From his role as an intern, to his position as the Director of Education, Tai has had an impact on the Association through his creative vision. His insight has helped to grow the educational program at the AFCA national convention to the premier professional development destination for the football coaching industry. Beyond that, his penchant for identifying talent has proven to be one of his greatest assets. This attribute of his character has helped him to become a successful entrepreneur.

Those accomplishments, however, pale in comparison to his power of influence. I am most impressed by Tai's commitment to providing opportunities for young professionals through servant leadership and professional development. Although you just finished reading about how he goes about accomplishing this feat, I had the pleasure of watching him do it firsthand with a young man who would enter our organization just 10 years later.

Lightning rarely strikes in the same place twice. Moreover, I could have never forecasted it happening under my watch in an intimate office setting of less than 20 people. Again, I was humbled. In 2012, lightning once again took on human form, when Tai introduced me to his new graduate assistant, Will Baggett. I could sense the instant chemistry between Will and Tai. Their synergistic vigor was palpable and filled every nook and cranny of my office. After comparing the look in Will's eyes with the one Tai held, it became immediately clear to me that these guys were real treasures, absolute gems. Although their personalities differ, their work ethic, passion, and shared commitment to helping others are mirror images of one another and are reflected in the preceding text. By the end of Will's first semester at Baylor, he was already recommending a fellow student for a graduate assistant position that had not yet been created.

Within a month, we implemented this assistantship and successfully filled the position with Will's recommendation, eventually hiring her on full-time. This occurrence was but a microcosm of things to come, and Will has not looked back since. He went on to create the Baylor Sport Management Association to facilitate opportunities for his fellow students and was later named the 2014 Outstanding Graduate of his program. He became an invaluable asset and remains a devoted volunteer for the American Football Coaches Association's annual convention. Not unlike Tai, I am most pleased with the person he is and the professional he has become, in turn.

Nevertheless, my only lingering regret after leading both Will and Tai is that others did not have the benefit of seeing what I saw on a daily basis. Then again, maybe you have now seen the picture just as clearly after reading the preceding lines. Similar to a blueprint, such lines are merely designed to present an illustration of things to come. But as we all know, this is only the beginning of…the process.

—Grant Teaff
College Football Hall of Fame

Share the Book

If you enjoyed *The Blueprint*, share it with someone!

Connect with us on Twitter @W_BaggsCFP and @TaiMBrown. Be sure to post your copy on any social media platform using the hashtag #TheBlueprint.

For speaking engagements or consulting inquiries, we may be reached at:

Will@execimage.org
BrownTai@gmail.com

ABOUT THE AUTHORS

William C. Baggett

Will Baggett was born and raised on the outskirts of Grenada, Mississippi. His parents, Bill and Maggie Baggett, have lived in Oxford, Mississippi, since 2011. At the tender age of six, Will's father picked up on his unique affinity for words after hearing him recite the entire script of the movie *Street Fighter* (1994). His dad recalls sitting in utter disbelief as his first grader recited each actor's lines verbatim for the duration of the film. The hidden duality of this experience would gradually begin to play itself out over the course of Will's life and career.

Will excelled in the classroom throughout his academic tenure, culminating in graduations from both the University of Mississippi and Baylor University, with Magna Cum Laude honors. It was under the tutelage of an instructor he met as a junior in high school, however, that would set the trajectory for Will's career as a writer. In fall 2006, he entered the classroom of the late Mrs. Charlene Leverette for the first time. Terrified by the urban legend surrounding her course's difficulty, Will and his fellow students sat in silence until she broke the proverbial ice as only she could. Without uttering a word, she grabbed an idle broomstick, straddled it, and proceeded to gallop around the classroom as her new pupils stared in astonishment.

Upon completing the ride and dismounting her trusty steed, Mrs. Leverette made eye contact with an awestricken Will and began her public address to the classroom. "You all probably think I'm crazy by now, don't you? Well, don't just sit there. Write about it!" And so he did. He wrote his way to near the top of his cohort, developing a penchant for poetry and an uncanny ability to tie abstract concepts to real life principles. Will credits her with helping to instill an unbridled confidence within him and cultivating his distinctive style. Unfortunately, that academic year would prove to be the last ride for Will with Mrs. Leverette at the reigns as she would opt for retirement in the summer of 2007. Distraught, Will discontinued writing altogether and declined to enroll in the follow-up course.

After completing his undergraduate degree at University of Mississippi, he went on to Baylor University and landed a graduate assistantship at the American Football Coaches Association, under the direction of Tai M. Brown. This work relationship would quickly develop into a brotherhood, as the two became joined at the hip. Side by side, the tandem traveled near and far gathering new experiences, while learning from one another every step of the way.

Tai, already a professional development savant, readily shared his insights and passion for developing young people as he began to pour into Will's life. Through a sort of osmosis, Will soon adopted this passion and began documenting his experiences as a young professional as Tai led the way.

It was through routine writing assignments that Tai began to take notice of Will's unique writing ability. Will, however, admittedly stubborn at the time, paid it no mind. After two years under Tai's watch, with a graduate degree in hand, Will set out to begin his own career in Atlanta, Georgia.

In less than 90 days, Will had taken notice of the systemic, widening gap between young professionals and their tenured counterparts. Anxious to begin bridging this gap, Will put in a call to Tai in search of an outlet to articulate all he had gleaned under Tai's leadership. Again, Tai cited Will's penchant for the written word and mentioned how their shared passion for professional development could serve as the vehicle. Although Will had not written for personal edification since Mrs. Leverette's retirement, this time he listened, and so *The Blueprint* came to be.

As a talented freelance actor, Will enjoys having his own lines to recite nowadays, having appeared in a number of plays and hit television shows. He now resides in Dallas, Texas, and enjoys volunteering at his local church, collecting various currencies, and reading.

Tai M. Brown

Tai M. Brown was born and raised in Inglewood, California. His mother, Teri M. Brown, served in a trifecta of trades as a special education teacher, dean of students, and athletics director in the Los Angeles Unified School District. Tai's father, Larry Brown, was also an employee of the school district, serving in various roles within the school system.

Although both of his parents hailed from the state of Michigan, they would not find one another until meeting in Los Angeles in the mid-70s. His parents went on to enjoy 20 years of marriage. In 1997, just after his freshman year of college, Tai's father succumbed to health complications, stemming from the side effects of addiction. A proud "mama's boy," Tai lost his mother in 2016 not long after the publication of this book.

After high school, Tai went on to Michigan State University. It was during his freshman year that Tai tried out for the football team but failed to make the final cut. Undeterred, he went through tryouts again as a sophomore and ultimately earned a spot on the Spartans' football roster.

Equipped with an uncanny work ethic, Tai remained as a non-scholarship student-athlete for two seasons, while under the tutelage of head coach, Nick Saban. During his senior year, he was fortuitously awarded an athletic scholarship with the help of his position coach Mark Dantonio and newly minted head coach, Bobby Williams. Tai went on to graduate with dual bachelor's degrees in finance and information technology. Following graduation, he worked as an office assistant at a commercial real estate office (Kilroy Realty) in Los Angeles for one year.

Feeling the tug to get back into sports, particularly football, Tai one day happened upon an advertisement for an internship in sport administration at the American Football Coaches Association (AFCA). He satisfied the requirement of gaining admission to Baylor University and proceeded to begin his tenure under former NFL player, and AFCA Director of Education, Walter Abercrombie.

Walter mentored Tai on the tenets of professionalism and quickly planted the seed of servant-leadership. In 2004, Abercrombie opted for a position with his alma mater Baylor University, leaving Tai to fill the gap in AFCA's Education Division. Anxious to plug the developmental divot of Abercrombie's absence, he began crafting his organizational leadership principles by studying the football coaches he served.

Soon after, eager to try his hand at implementing these principles, he began hiring students at the AFCA on a part-time basis. Over time, however, the need for continuity became vital, so he decided to bring in a graduate assistant who could stay on for two years. In 2012, Will Baggett surfaced to satisfy this need, marking the start of their storied relationship. In that same year, Tai became a small business owner by establishing Spades Media Group-Roots of Wisdom, LLC with the purpose of *solving problems using creative leadership strategies*.

His work in football, education, and developing young professionals has culminated in *Forward Management©*, an organizational leadership philosophy, implemented through Spades, that helps leaders create a productive and enterprising environment. Spades provides a variety of services including staffing athletic events, media production, and leadership/management consulting.

Tai is an ardent supporter of family and friends, as well as a personal and professional development enthusiast. His friends and colleagues consider him a problem-solver, and he works assiduously to ensure the success of everyone around him. His brother, Everette, lives in Los Angeles. Tai is also an avid Bob Marley fan and considers Marley's song, *Three Little Birds*, to be an ode to him and his two sisters, Shāāla and Ketia.